First Workshop on Natural Language Processing Tools and Resources for Translation and Interpreting Applications (NLP4TIA 2023)

Varna, Bulgaria
8 September 2023

ISBN: 978-1-7138-9059-1

Printed from e-media with permission by:

Curran Associates, Inc.
57 Morehouse Lane
Red Hook, NY 12571

Some format issues inherent in the e-media version may also appear in this print version.

Printed with permission by Curran Associates, Inc. (2025)

For permission requests, please contact the Association for Computational Linguistics at the address below.

Association for Computational Linguistics
209 N. Eighth Street
Stroudsburg, Pennsylvania 18360

Phone: 1-570-476-8006
Fax: 1-570-476-0860

acl@aclweb.org

Additional copies of this publication are available from:

Curran Associates, Inc.
57 Morehouse Lane
Red Hook, NY 12571 USA
Phone: 845-758-0400
Fax: 845-758-2633
Email: curran@proceedings.com
Web: www.proceedings.com

NLP4TIA 2023

First Workshop
on Natural Language Processing tools and resources
for translation and interpreting applications

associated with
The 14th International Conference on
Recent Advances in Natural Language Processing'2023

PROCEEDINGS

Edited by Raquel Lázaro Gutiérrez, Marie Escribe, Teodora Mihajlov,
Maria Kunilovskaya, and Ruslan Mitkov

Varna, Bulgaria
8 September, 2023
https://nlp4tia.web.uah.es/

First Workshop on Natural Language Processing tools and resources for translation and interpreting applications (NLP4TIA)
Associated with the International Conference
Recent Advances in Natural Language Processing'2023

PROCEEDINGS

8 September, 2023
https://nlp4tia.web.uah.es

e-book site: www.acl-bg.org

INCOMA Ltd.
Shoumen, BULGARIA

Sponsors:

Organising Committee & Workshop Chairs:

Raquel Lázaro-Gutiérrez (Universidad de Alcalá, Spain)
Antonio Pareja-Lora (Universidad de Alcalá, Spain)
Ruslan Mitkov (Lancaster University)
Marie Escribe (Polytechnic University of Valencia & LanguageWire, Spain)
Maria Kunilovskaya (Saarland University, Germany)
Teodora Mihajlov (Univeristy of Belgrade, Serbia)
Khadija Ait ElFqih (University of Naples l'Orientale, Italy)
Andrés Felipe Herrera Ramírez (Universidad de Alcalá, Spain)

Programme Committee:

Fabio Alves Federal (Federal University of Minas Gerais)
William Lewis (University of Washington)
Juanjo Arevalillo (Hermes Traducciones)
Silvia Bernardini (University of Bologna)
Gabriel Cabrera Méndez (Dualia Teletraducciones)
Matt Coler (University of Groningen)
Gloria Corpas Pastor (University of Malaga)
Elena Davitti (University of Surrey)
Joanna Drugan (Heriot-Watt University)
Marie Escribe (Polytechnic University of Valencia & LanguageWire, Spain)
Claudio Fantinuoli (Mainz University/KUDO Inc)
Antonio García Cabot (University of Alcalá)
Adriana Jaime Pérez (Migralingua Voze)
Miguel Ángel Jiménez Crespo (Rutgers University)
Koen Kerremans (Free University Brussel)
Maria Kunilovskaya (Saarland University)

Els Lefever (Ghent University)
Pilar León Arauz (University of Granada)
Johanna Monti (University of Naples L'Orientale)
Elena Montiel Ponsoda (Polytecnic University Madrid)
Helena Moriz (University of Lisbon)
Elena Murgolo (Orbital 14)
Dora Murgu (Interprefy)
Constantin Orasan (University of Surrey)
María Teresa Ortego Antón (University of Valladolid)
Tharindu Ranasinghe (Aston University)
Celia Rico (Universidad Complutense de Madrid)
Caroline Rossi (University Grenoble les Alpes)
María del Mar Sánchez Ramos (University of Alcalá)
Miriam Seghiri (University of Malaga)
Vilelmini Sosoni (Ionian University)
Rui Manuel Sousa Silva (University of Porto)
Nicoletta Spinolo (University of Bologna)

Table of Contents

Natural Language Processing tools and resources for translation and interpreting applications

Introduction

Raquel Lázaro Gutiérrez

Universidad de Alcalá
raquel.lazaro@uah.es

In the last two decades we have been able to witness a technological turn in translation and interpreting studies with natural language processing (NLP) and deep learning playing more and more prominent part. There is a growing number of NLP applications which are used to support the work of translators and interpreters. The emergence of highly successful deep learning models resulted in very promising Neural Machine Translation (NMT) performance.

Jiménez Crespo (2021) reflects on the reality and discernability of a disciplinary turn in translation both as a profession and a field of research. After reviewing the concepts of "turn" and "technological turn" as defined, amongst others, by well-known translation scholars, such as Sin-Wai (2004), Cronin (2010) or O'Hagan (2013), Jiménez Crespo describes this phenomenon as "a process by which translation theories begin to incorporate the increasingly evident impact of technology, developing theoretical tools and frameworks for translation studies and related disciplines". Human-computer interaction is nowadays a common practice and situation in professional translation (O'Brien 2012). Corpus analysis, terminology management, computer assisted translation tools, machine translation, translation project management software are at the core of the profession.

The translation technology revolution has transformed the translation profession and nowadays most professional translators employ tools such as translation memory (TM) systems in their daily work. Latest advances of Neural Machine Translation (NBT) has resulted in NMT not only becoming an integral part of most state-of-the art TM tools but also typical for the translation workflow of many companies and organisations.

Although translation has benefited more from technological advances, interpreting has also experienced a technological turn. Fantinuoli (2018) points out that technology has been present in professional interpretation since the beginning of simultaneous interpreting systems in 1920s. Technology mediated interpreting has also been popular in dialogue settings, and telephone interpreting dates back to the 1950s (Braun, 2015; Cabrera Méndez, 2016). However, it has not been until some years ago that soft technology has permeated interpreting practice and research. Computer assisted translation, MT and NLP tools have been adapted to be used by interpreters. One of the most important related projects is VIP (Corpas Pastor, 2021), a platform that integrates several CAI tools (terminology management, speech-to-text, note-taking).

Shlesinger (1998) already mentioned several decades ago the benefits of using corpus-based methodologies in interpreting studies, particularly to obtain information about lexical, grammatical or discursive patterns. Authors such as Van Besien (1999), Takagi et al. (2002) or Ryu et al. (2003) pioneered corpus-based studies on simultaneous conference interpreting, focusing on interpreting techniques, time span or contrastive linguistic features respectively.

More recently, corpus-based studies have reached dialogue interpreting. For instance, the ComInDat Pilot Corpus (Angermeyer, Meyer and Schmidt, 2012) comprised two subcorpora of interpreter-mediated medical interviews and court trials.

Proceedings of the First NLP4TIA Workshop, pages 1–3
Varna, Sep 8, 2023
https://doi.org/10.26615/978-954-452-091-5_001

More recent are the corpora TIPp, which also contains interpreter-mediated court trials, and INTELPRAGMA / PRAGMACOR, made of telephone interpreter-mediated interactions (Himoro and Pareja-Lora, 2022). Most of the corpora of dialogue interpretations have been processed and analysed with the software EXMARaLDA.

The increasing interest in NLP and the automation of processes has brought us to multidisciplinary projects that deal with the development of models for automated oral communication. Machine interpreting has already been developed and is being improved, focusing on speed and accuracy matters (Müller et al. 2016). Either domain-specific (commercial, military, humanitarian…) or general (Skype Translator), there is still a long way to go to render machine interpreting more human-like (Braun, 2019).

The eight contributions contained in this volume are rich and varied. Machine translation is profusely tackled, with a special emphasis on under resourced languages and combinations, such as Ngambay-French or Romanian-Spanish, and literary translation, a field in which neural machine translation and generative pre-trained transformer models are contributing to improve quality and smooth the translation workflow. Pre-trained transformer models are also approached in this volume, not only to experiment in their design for specific challenges, such as idioms, but also to evaluate their usefulness at different stages of the translation workflow, such as the revision phase.

In sum, this volume offers cutting-edge studies revolving around artificial intelligence, NLP and large language models in relation to both translation and interpreting, presenting innovative research results while opening new paths to further experimentation.

References

Alfred. V. Aho and Jeffrey D. Ullman. 1972. *The Theory of Parsing, Translation and Compiling, volume 1*. Prentice-Hall, Englewood Cliffs, NJ.

Philip Angermeyer, Bernd Meyer, B., and Thomas Schmidt. 2012. Sharing community interpreting corpora. In Thomas Schmidt, T., and Kai Wörner, K. (eds.) *Multilingual Corpora and Multilingual Corpus Analysis*. Amsterdam: John Benjamins, pages 275-294.

Sabine Braun. 2015. Remote interpreting. In Holly Mikkelson, and Renée Jourdenais (Eds) *The Routledge Handbook of Interpreting*. London/New York: Routledge, pages 352-367.

Sabine Braun. 2019. Technology and interpreting. In Minako O'Hagan (Ed.) *The Routledge Handbook of Translation and Technology*. London: Routledge, pages 271-288.

Gabriel Cabrera Méndez. 2016. *Mamá, quiero ser intérprete*. Madrid: Pie de Página Editorial.

Gloria Corpas Pastor. 2021. Technology Solutions for Interpreters: The VIP System. *Hermēneus. Revista de Traducción e Interpretación*, 23: 91-123.

Michael Cronin. 2010. Globalization and translation. In Yves Gambier, and Luc van Doorslaer (eds.) *Handbook of Translation Studies. Volume 1*. Amsterdam: John Benjamins, pages 134-140.

Claudio Fantinuoli. 2018. Interpreting and technology. The upcoming technological turn. In Claudio Fantinuoli (ed.) 2018. Interpreting and Technology. Berlin: Language Science Press, pages 1-12.

Marcelo Yuji Himoro, and Antonio Pareja-Lora. 2022. Codificación y anotación preliminar de un corpus oral multilingüe de conversaciones telefónicas interpretadas para el estudio de los ataques a la imagen. *Pragmalingüística*, (30): 413–432.

Miguel Ángel Jiménez Crespo. 2021. Localization. In Esperança Bielsa, and Dionysios Kapsaskis (eds.) The Routledge Handbook of Translation and Globalization. London: Routledge, pages 392-405.

Markus Müller, Thai Son Nguyen, Jan Niehues, Eunah Cho, Bastian Krüger, Thanh-Le Ha, Kevin Kilgour, Matthias Sperber, Mohammed Mediani, Sebastian Stüker, and Alex Waibel. 2016. Lecture Translator - Speech translation framework for simultaneous lecture translation. In *Proceedings of the 2016 Conference of the North American Chapter of the Association for Computational Linguistics: Demonstrations*, San Diego, California. Association for Computational Linguistics, pages 82–86.

Sharon O'Brien. 2012. Translation as human–computer interaction. *Translation Spaces*, 1: 101–122.

Minako O'Hagan. 2013. The Impact of New Technologies on Translation Studies:A technological turn? In Carmen Millán, and Francesca Bartrina. *The Routledge Handbook of Translation Studies*, London: Routledge, pages 503-518.

Koichiro Ryu, Shigeki Matsubara, Nobuo Kawaguchi, and Yasuyoshi Inagaki, Y. 2003. Bilingual Speech Dialogue Corpus for Simultaneous Machine Interpretation Research. In *Proceedings of the 6th Oriental COCOSDA workshop in Singapore on Oct 1-3 2003*, pages164-168.

Miriam Shlesinger. 1998. Corpus-Based Interpreting Studies as an Offshoot of Corpus-Based Translation Studies. *Meta*, 43(4): 486-493.

Chan Sin-Wai. 2004. *A Dictionary of Translation Technology*. Hong Kong: The Chinese University Press.

Akira Takagi, Shigeki Matsubara, and Yasuyoshi Inagaki. 2002. A corpus-based analysis of simultaneous interpretation. In *Proceedings of International Joint Conference of the 5th Symposium on Natural Language Processing (SNLP-2002)*, pages 167-174.

Fred Van Besien. 1999. Anticipation in Simultaneous Interpretation. Meta 44(2): 250-259.

Machine translation, translation errors, and adequacy: Spanish-English vs. Spanish-Romanian

Laura Monguilod
lauramong@hotmail.com
Bianca Vitalaru
bianca.vitalaru@uah.es
Universidad de Alcalá

Abstract

This paper has two objectives: 1. To analyse the adequacy of using neural machine translation (NMT) for the translation of health information (from Spanish into English and Romanian) used in Spanish public health campaigns; and 2. To compare results considering these two linguistic combinations. Results show that post-editing is essential to improve the quality of the translations for both language combinations since they cannot be used as a primary resource for informing foreign users without post-editing. Moreover, Romanian translations require more post-editing. However, using NMT for informative texts combined with human post-editing can be used as a strategy to benefit from the potential of MT while at the same time ensuring the quality of the public service translations depending on the language combination and on the amount of time allotted for the task.

1 Introduction

Within the context of globalisation and crisis situations characterised by the increase of the migrants' percentage in Europe, Spain's foreign population kept growing in the last decade. In fact, it increased by 182,141 people in the first half of 2022 (INE, 2022). This situation has affected both the general needs for social integration and access to public services (i.e., education, administration, healthcare, or social welfare) and specifically the communication needs to access these rights in several language pairs. On the other hand, as Navaza, Estévez, and Serrano (2009) underline, healthcare providers who needed to be able to inform patients who did not understand Spanish were also affected. One of the foreign populations that maintained its percentage in the last decade in Spain is the Romanian population (See, for example, that it had more than 600.000 people every year since 2008 according to INE, 1998-2022).

In the specific context of the healthcare settings, as one of the rights that the foreign population has, health campaigns are used as a tool to transmit essential information regarding healthcare to the general population, usually focusing on disease prevention or situations that can imply some level of risk. They also include or even specifically address the foreign population, who, due to communication difficulties or cultural differences, may not be aware of the risks they are exposed to and of the prevention measures that they should take. In fact, both linguistic and cultural differences can hinder the dissemination of healthcare-related materials (Sixsmith et al., 2014).

On the other hand, technology in general can assist in the provision of (public) services to both the general and the foreign population and facilitates the provision of services that were previously unavailable (Sánchez Ramos & Rico Pérez, 2020). Technology is also fundamental in the translation and interpreting (T&I) sector,

Proceedings of the First NLP4TIA Workshop, pages 4–12
Varna, Sep 8, 2023
https://doi.org/10.26615/978-954-452-091-5_002

which is the channel that facilitates communication when the foreign population is involved. This channel is specifically relevant within the Public Service Interpreting and Translation (PSIT) context, that is, fields such as education, administration, social welfare, healthcare, and legal settings (Sánchez Ramos & Rico Pérez, 2020; Valero-Garcés, 2018), to which the foreign population has free access. Additionally, within the private T&I sector, technologies (especially CAT tools and including Machine Translation (MT) and post-editing) are an essential part of translators' daily work to reduce costs, increase efficiency, and improve productivity (Sánchez Ramos & Rico Pérez, 2020). Moreover, if an effective post-editing process is followed, the use of MT or terminology management tools can improve productivity, assist with textual consistency, and ensure better quality (Sánchez Ramos & Rico Pérez, 2020). Furthermore, some other advantages should be considered, such as the fact that CAT tools allow the translator to store their work so that they can use it again when they need to work with similar texts (Kerremans et al., 2018). However, the use of technology (especially MT), also generates debates among professionals regarding the quality of the product obtained due to "terminological inconsistencies, false meanings, and a clear lack of syntactic and stylistic systematicity" (Kerremans et al., 2018). Finally, specialists have also been reluctant to incorporate translation tools in migrant support contexts (Sánchez Ramos & Rico Pérez, 2020).

Considering this context, this paper has two objectives:

1. To analyse the adequacy of using neural machine translation (NMT) for the translation of health information (from Spanish into English and Romanian) used in Spanish public health campaigns.
2. To compare results considering the Spanish-English (ES-EN) and the Spanish-Romanian (ES-RO) combinations.

We based this study on two hypotheses: 1) NMT outputs are not completely adequate if used as a primary resource for informing foreign users without post-editing and 2) there will be more translation errors in the Spanish-Romanian combination than in the Spanish-English combination, which will, in turn, require more post-editing.

2 Classifying translation errors: human and machine translation

A translation error can be defined as an inappropriate equivalence (Hurtado Albir, 2011). Translation errors are directly related to translation problems (Hurtado Albir, 2011) especially because translation problems are seldom found in the translation process (Gregorio Cano, 2017) and can be identified in advance. In addition, they are different from translation difficulties since they do not depend on the translator's ability to solve problems as an individual (Nord, 2007).

Translation errors are fundamental when analysing and evaluating translation quality and can be classified based on different criteria. The most frequent categories one can find when defining and analysing translation errors are related to errors concerning either the source text or the target language and the two main phases of translation: comprehension and re-expression (Hurtado Albir, 2011). Moreover, the type of translator (human or MT) is another criterion to be considered. In fact, we believe that to identify the types of errors and analyse them correctly we need to be aware of the similarities and differences between the outputs of both types of translators. That is why we show, in Table 1, a list and a basic comparison between two classifications of translation errors:

Common human translation errors (Delisle, 1993, cited in Hurtado Albir, 2011)	**Common MT errors** (Alarcón Navío, 2003)
False sense. Countermeaning. Nonsense.	False meanings. Nonsenses. Terminological improprieties. Syntactic and lexical calques of the source language.
Addition.	-
Omission. Hypertranslation. Overtranslation. Undertranslation.	Untranslated words. Repetitions. Unnecessary foreign words. Alteration of word order and punctuation. Incorrect use of prepositions and verb tenses. Incorrect translation of double negation. Errors in the translation of lexicalised metaphors.

Table 1: Classification of translation errors

Considering that this research focuses on the use of NMT, we will provide the characteristics for the types of MT errors whose meaning might require some clarification (as stated by Alarcón Navío, 2003) and the list that will be used to identify translation errors in our study:

- False meanings: hinder text comprehension by choosing a term that can be considered similar but is incorrect.

- Nonsenses: a consequence of discursive incoherence and syntactic structures that are difficult to understand. According to Vázquez and del Arbol (2008), two types of nonsense are particularly significant: on the one hand, [simple] nonsense, understood as a mistake that can hinder text comprehension, and complete nonsense words/expressions, understood as a type of nonsense that renders the discourse meaningless and illogical.

- Terminological improprieties: the target term that has been chosen is not quite adequate since the most general definition of the term has been used.

- Syntactic and lexical calques of the source language: borrowing word order and structures from the source language.

- Untranslated words: using the source terms instead of translations.

- Unnecessary foreign words: using unnecessary loans.

- Others: repetitions, alterations of word order or punctuation, incorrect use of prepositions or verb tenses, incorrect translation of double negations, errors in the translation of lexicalised metaphors.

3 Methodology

The methodology used to obtain information is descriptive and it involves corpus compilation, error tagging using MT and the Raw Output Evaluator tool, as well as counting and analysing translation errors.

Specifically, we took the following steps:

1. Corpus compilation of texts from three health campaigns of the Spanish Ministry of Health (see Table 2). The texts were chosen considering the importance of healthcare campaigns for prevention and healthcare purposes in general and their specific role when it comes to informing the foreign population on disease prevention or situations that imply some level of risk. Ultimately, we also kept in mind the fact that linguistic and cultural differences have been found to hinder the distribution of healthcare-related materials (Álvaro Aranda, 2020).

Campaign	**Nº of words**
1. Malos Humos	206
2. Alcohol	148
3. Conducta suicida	185

Table 2: Corpus

2. Feeding the texts of the campaigns to two free online MT engines: DeepL and Google Translator (GT) and using the translations to create a translations corpus for each language (English and Romanian). Free online MT engines were chosen for two main reasons: the fact that free tools are available and widely used nowadays, especially by trainees and the current scarcity or even lack of funds to provide PSIT services in Spain. From this point of view, our basic analysis of the situation showed that associations, NGO, and organisations that usually provide social or economic assistance to the foreign population usually rely on little financial help regarding linguistic assistance. Thus, they need to turn to free tools. By analysing these engines, we can have an insight into the MT that can be used by organisations for which these MT are the only available options and the contexts in which they could be used.

3. Uploading the translations corpora to the Raw Output Evaluator tool.

4. Identifying and tagging translation errors in the corpora of translations available within the Raw Output Evaluator tool. To determine the errors, we applied Alarcón Navío's (2003) classification of common MT errors (see Table 1). The Raw Output Evaluator is a tool that helps the user to compare several translations at once. These translations can either be generated within the tool or can be uploaded to the tool and the types of errors must be manually tagged by the user. The tool can also be

used during the post-editing process, and it allows the classification of the different types of errors found when using MT (Farrell, 2018).

5. Analysing the types of errors in context and counting the number of errors.

6. Evaluating the adequacy of the outputs considering the types of translation errors previously established and the percentage of errors. We relied on Reiss's (1983) definition of adequacy, which is based on "appropriateness". We first considered that the translation was adequate when it was considered appropriate in a specific medical, social, and cultural context/setting. Additionally, we also kept in mind the number of translation errors found in relation to the total number of words of the corpus compiled.

7. Comparing the results considering the English and the Romanian corpora.

4 Results

We chose three campaigns to test our hypotheses and show our results and several examples of translation errors have been included by type of error in Table 3 and Table 4.

MT errors	Original text (ES)	DeepL (EN)	GT (EN)
False meanings	*Disfrutar de un entorno saludable es primordial. No fumar tabaco ni relacionados lo hace posible, por eso di ¿MALOS HUMOS? NO, GRACIAS*	Enjoying a healthy environment is paramount. Not smoking tobacco or related makes it possible, that's why I said BAD SMOKES? NO, THANKS	Enjoying a healthy environment is paramount. Not smoking tobacco or related products makes it possible, so say NO SMOKE? NO, THANK YOU
Syntactic and lexical calques of the source languages	*Disfrutar de un entorno saludable es primordial. No fumar tabaco ni relacionados lo hace posible, por eso di ¿MALOS HUMOS? NO, GRACIAS*	Enjoying a healthy environment is paramount. Not smoking tobacco or related makes it possible, that's why I said BAD SMOKES? NO, THANKS	Enjoying a healthy environment is paramount. Not smoking tobacco or related products makes it possible, so say NO SMOKE? NO, THANK YOU
Terminological improprieties/imprecise expressions	*La mejor opción es dejarlo, y si no lo has hecho aún, respeta en esos espacios a los demás, especialmente a personas vulnerables.*	The best option is to leave it, and if you haven't done it yet, respect others in those spaces, especially vulnerable people.	The best option is to quit, and if you have not already done so, respect others in these spaces, especially vulnerable people.
Repetitions	*Estudios recientes señalan que un número creciente de hombres gais, bisexuales y otros hombres que tienen relaciones sexuales con hombres (GBHSH) tiene el VIH.*	Recent studies indicate that a growing number of gay, bisexual, and other men who have sex with men (GBHSM) men have HIV.	Recent studies indicate that a growing number of gay, bisexual and other men who have sex with men (GBHSH) have HIV.
Lexicalised metaphors	*EL HUMO NO TE DEJA VER.*	THE SMOKE DOES NOT LET YOU SEE.	SMOKE IS BLIND.

Table 3: Examples of the types of errors found in the English translations

MT errors	Original text (ES) [authors' English translation]	DeepL (RO) [authors' English translation]	GT (RO)

Syntactic and lexical calques of the source languages False meanings	*El Ministerio de Sanidad promueve la Línea 024 de atención a la conducta suicida* [The Ministry of Health promotes the 024-Suicide line to assist people with suicidal behaviours].	Ministerul Sănătății promovează linia telefonică 024 pentru suicid [The Ministry of Health promotes the 024-telephone line for suicide].	Ministerul Sănătății promovează Linia fierbinte 024 pentru atenția asupra comportamentului suicidar. [The Ministry of Health promotes the 024 Hotline for attention towards suicidal behaviour].
Terminological improprieties/imprecise expressions	*Somos uno de los países con más vacunados: el 93% de la población mayor de 12 años se ha administrado la pauta completa de primovacunación* [We are one of the countries with the highest number of vaccinated people: 93% of the population over the age of 12 has received the full primary vaccination series].	Suntem una dintre cele mai vaccinate țări din lume: 93% din populația cu vârsta de peste 12 ani a primit vaccinarea primară completă [We are one of the world's most vaccinated countries: 93% of the population over the age of 12 has received the full primary vaccination].	Suntem una dintre țările cu cele mai vaccinate: 93% din populația cu vârsta peste 12 ani a primit programul complet de vaccinare primară [We are one of the countries with the most vaccinated*: 93% of the population over the age of 12 has received the full primary vaccination programme].
	Lo importante es no participar [The important thing is to not participate].	Este important să nu participați [It is important not to participate].	Important este să nu participi [What matters is that you do not participate].

Table 4: Examples of errors found in the Romanian translations

Four aspects were particularly significant. First, we found significant examples in terms of the changing of the meaning as a result of syntactic and lexical calques and false meanings: e.g., the literal translation for "El Ministerio de Sanidad promueve la Línea 024 de atención a la conducta suicida" was 1) "Ministerul Sănătății promovează linia telefonică 024 pentru suicid" [translation of the Romanian version: "The Ministry of Health promotes the telephone line 024 for suicide"] (DeepL) and 2) "Ministerul Sănătății promovează Linia fierbinte 024 pentru atenția asupra comportamentului suicidar" [translation of the Romanian version: "The Ministry of Health promotes the Hot line 024 for attention towards suicidal behaviour". The underlined words in the original translation and the translation of the Romanian version show that the meaning was completely changed in both cases. Second, both engines failed to be coherent when choosing the target terms throughout the same text, changing for no apparent reason since the same context was applicable. This is the case of "autocita-autocite-selfquote-selfappointment" (in the English corpus) and of several inconsistencies between the formal and informal way of addressing the reader (in the Romanian corpus). Third, we found several translation errors for examples of everyday language (e.g., related to smoking). Finally, the translation of metaphors (e.g., campaña 'Malos Humos' ['Smoking Is Bad' Campaign]; 'El Humo No Te Deja Ver' ['Smoke Blinds You']) has also been a challenge for both languages, especially for DeepL in the case of the English translations and for GT in the case of the Romanian translations.

Finally, we included the types of MT errors we found in the analysis of the DeepL and GT outputs for both language combinations and their frequency in Table 5:

Campaign (ES)	**Nº of words**	**Type of error**	**DeepL (EN)**	**GT (EN)**	**DeepL (RO)**	**GT (RO)**
1. Malos Humos	206	False meanings	2	2	4	6

		Syntactic and lexical calques and lexicalised metaphors	3	2	6	5
		Terminological improprieties			3	1
		Grammar mistakes				1
		Unnecessary foreign words or no translations				1
		Repetitions				
2. Alcohol	148	False meanings				3
		Syntactic and lexical calques and lexicalised metaphors	1	0	1	2
		Terminological improprieties			2	2
		Grammar mistakes				1
3. Conducta suicida	185	False meanings			1	1
		Syntactic and lexical calques and lexicalised metaphors		1		1
		Terminological improprieties	1	0	3	4
		Grammar mistakes				1
		Unnecessary foreign words or no translations				
		Repetitions				1

Table 5: Number of errors by type of text

Furthermore, Table 6 shows a comparative summary of the number and types of translation errors in both language combinations and using both translation engines. We found a variety of translation errors (nine types grouped in eight categories) of the list we established in section 2 and different results considering the two translation engines and the two language combinations involved. In this case, the Romanian translations had translation errors from all the categories included in Table 1 for both translation engines while the English translations had errors for six of the eight categories included. We also found more translation errors in the case of the Spanish-Romanian combination.

Type of error	**DeepL (EN)**	**GT (EN)**	**DeepL (RO)**	**GT (RO)**
False meanings	5	3	15	28
Syntactic and lexical calques and lexicalised metaphors	5	3	17	30
Terminological improprieties/imprecise expressions	3	0	20	26
Grammar mistakes	2	3	5	11
Omissions	2	1	1	1
Loans or no translation	0	0	2	7
Repetitions	1	0	1	2
Spelling mistakes	0	0	1	4

Table 6: Summary of the types of errors

Finally, we determined the percentage of translation errors considering the total number of words in the texts we analysed (539 words) and shown in Table 7. In general, they were below 3.5% in the English translations and not higher we observed that the percentage was much higher in the Spanish-Romanian combination than in the case of the Spanish-English combination, as than 20% in the Romanian translations:

	DeepL (EN)	GT (EN)	DeepL (RO)	GT (RO)
Total number of errors	18	10	62	109
%	3.33%	1.85%	11.5%	20%

Table 7. Percentage of translation errors

5 Discussions

Results show both similarities and differences considering the types of translation errors and the number of errors in the two language combinations involved considering the translations produced specifically in informative texts from health campaigns.

First, we observed that MT involved a variety of translation errors in these types of texts (see Tables 3, 4, and 5). The most common types of translation errors in both language combinations were false meanings, syntactic and lexical calques of the source language, terminological improprieties/lack of precision, grammar mistakes/errors, and the translation of lexicalised metaphors. We only found differences in the case of omissions and repetitions on the one hand (for the Spanish-English combination), and spelling mistakes and loans on the other hand (for the Spanish-Romanian combination).

Second, if we consider the results obtained for each engine and each language combination, we can underline several differences. The Romanian translations had more errors than the English translations in general. Moreover, in the case of the English translations, DeepL had more errors than GT, especially for terms with no context. On the opposite side, GT had more errors than DeepL in the Romanian translations, in some cases (false meanings and calques) with approx. 50% more errors in the GT output than in the DeepL output. In fact, all the Romanian texts included several examples of errors that hindered the correct transmission of the intended meaning: false meanings, syntactic and lexical calques of the source language, and terminological improprieties/imprecise expressions.

Therefore, although similar types of post-editing are required in both languages for adequacy purposes, there are important differences regarding the number of post-edits needed considering the two language combinations we compared. In this case, our results for informative texts from health campaigns suggest that the Romanian translations require much more post-editing than the English translations to achieve adequate results. Lastly, lack of coherence was also significant in both languages.

Third, despite the seriousness of the translation errors found in both language combinations and for both engines, the actual percentage of errors found was low considering the total number of words in the texts. This suggests that, although post-editing is required for adequate results that can be used to inform foreign users in a public setting, at least fragments of the texts translated are mostly functional. This means that the human effort required to apply post-editing strategies is generally low in both cases, especially for the English translations.

6 Conclusions

This study focused on the level of adequacy of the MT produced specifically in health campaigns' information and on the differences considering two language combinations.

The results we obtained helped us not only determine the level of adequacy of the translations for this type of texts but also reflect on their implications. Thus, if we refer to the transmission of information, the number of errors, and the seriousness of the translation errors, we could state that MT is only relatively adequate in the case of the English translations and not adequate in the case of Romanian translations. This verifies hypothesis 1, which suggests that MT alone is not adequate for the translation of informative health texts. Moreover, they showed that the number of translation errors and post-edits required is higher (and more varied) for the Spanish-Romanian combination, thus verifying hypothesis 2.

On the other hand, the results also made us reflect on the adequacy of using MT for informative texts combined with human post-editing as a strategy to benefit from the potential of MT while at the same time ensuring the quality of the public service translations. This strategy seems to depend on the language combination and on the amount of time allotted for the task. Therefore, English translations have a higher level of adequacy and potential since we found fewer translation errors and less error variety, which involves less post-editing time. In turn, Romanian translations have a lower level of adequacy since we found more translation errors and more error variety, which involves more post-editing time.

In general, considering the low percentage of translation errors in both language combinations, one could argue that these outputs can be defined as functional, considering that the main messages intended in the original texts can be understood, which is the main purpose when using MT. It seems that the translation engines analysed could be used as a starting point in the translation process of informative healthcare texts with adequate post-editing strategies and the post-editing would not require a great amount of time from the translator. This process is easier when healthcare informative texts are involved since they tend to be repetitive and NMT can rely on a great amount of information available online especially in language combinations that involve English.

However, we still have to keep in mind that, for the time being, MT engines cannot fully render the natural-sounding language that the human translation produces. In fact, as our analysis shows, despite their continuous development, both engines still had difficulties finding adequate translations for idiomatic expressions, metaphors, and even in the translation of everyday language and consistency in both language combinations. Therefore, human post-editing is still essential to achieve a completely functional and understandable text that is adequate from the linguistic, social, and medical points of view. Ultimately, MT translation will continue to be researched, specifically within the PSIT context and will continue to improve its quality. This means that the results with PSIT texts such as the ones analysed in this research will keep improving.

References

Alarcón Navío, Esperanza. (2003). *Traducción automática versus traducción humana: tipología de errores*. In Muñoz Martín, Ricardo (Ed.), I AIETI. Actas del I Congreso Internacional de la Asociación Ibérica de Estudios de Traducción e Interpretación, 2 (pp. 721-738). AIETI.

Álvaro Aranda, Cristina. (2020). La traducción de materiales sanitarios sobre la COVID-19 para población inmigrante: análisis exploratorio de propuestas en España. *TRANS: Revista de Traductología, 24*, 455-468. https://doi.org/10.24310/TRANS.2020.v0i24.9762

Farrell, Michael. (2018). Raw output evaluator, a freeware tool for manually assessing raw outputs from different machine translation engines. In *Proceedings of the 40th Conference Translating and the Computer* (pp. 38-49). Asling: International Society for Advancement in Language Technology.

Gregorio Cano, Ana. (2017). Problemas de traducción, detección y descripción: un estudio longitudinal en la formación de traductores. *Revista digital de investigación en docencia universitaria, 11*(2), 26-49. https://doi.org/10.19083/ridu.11.552

Hurtado Albir, Amparo. (2011). *Traducción y traductología. Introducción a la traductología.* (5°ed.). Ediciones Cátedra.

INE (2022). Cifras de Población a 1 de julio de 2022. Estadística de Migraciones (EM). Primer semestre de 2022. Notas de Prensa. https://www.ine.es/prensa/cp_j2022_p.pdf

INE (1998-2022). Población extranjera por nacionalidad, comunidades, sexo y año. https://www.ine.es/jaxi/Tabla.htm?path=/t20/e245/p08/l0/&file=02005.px&L=0

Kerremans, Koen, Lázaro Gutiérrez, Raquel, Stengers, Helene, Cox, Antoon, & Rillof, Pascal. (2019). Technology use by public service interpreters and translators: The link between frequency of use and forms of prior training. *FITISPos International Journal, 6*(1), 107-122.https://doi.org/10.37536/FITISPos-IJ.2019.6.1.211

Navaza, Bárbara, Estévez, Laura, & Serrano, Jordi, (2009). Saque la lengua, por favor. Panorama actual de la interpretación sanitaria en España. *Panace@, 10*(30), 141-156. https://dialnet.unirioja.es/servlet/articulo?codigo=3118253

Nord, Christiane. (2007). *Translating as a purposeful activity. Functionalist approaches explained. St. Jerome Publishing.*

Reiss, Katharina. (1983). Adequacy and equivalence in translation. *The Bible Translator, 34*(3), 301-308. https://doi.org/10.1177/026009358303400301

Sánchez Ramos, María del Mar., & Rico Pérez, Celia. (2020). *CRISIS-MT: traducción y tecnología en la comunicación multilingüe para las ONG en situaciones de emergencia*. Vicerrectorado de Investigación y Transferencia de la Universidad de Alcalá.

Sixsmith, Jane, Doyle, Priscilla, D'Earth Maureen, & Barry, Margaret M. (2014). *Health communication and its role in the prevention and control of communicable diseases in Europe. Current evidence, practice and future developments.* European Centre for Disease Prevention and Control.

Valero-Garces, Carmen. (2018). Introduction. PSIT and Technology. Challenges in the Digital Age. *FITISPos International Journal*, *5*(1), 1-6. https://doi.org/10.37536/FITISPos-IJ.2018.5.1.185

Vázquez y del Arbol, Esther. (2008). Aspectos de la traducción técnica: Errores e incorreciones graves en la traducción de manuales de instrucciones alemanes e italianos al español. *Lebende Sprachen* *53*(1), 2-6. https://doi.org/10.1515/LES.2008.2

Cross-Lingual Idiom Sense Clustering in German and English

Mohammed Shayaan Absar
absarshayaan@gmail.com

Abstract

Idioms are expressions with non-literal and non-compositional meanings. For this reason, they pose a unique challenge for various NLP tasks including Machine Translation and Sentiment Analysis. In this paper, we propose an approach to clustering idioms in different languages by their sense. We leverage pre-trained cross-lingual transformer models and fine-tune them to produce cross-lingual vector representations of idioms according to their sense.

1 Introduction

Idiom handling is an important aspect of any NLP system due to the unique way idioms can affect the meaning of a sentence. Due to their non-compositional meanings, NLP systems need to treat idioms as a single lexical unit. In Machine Translation, in particular, current transformer models tend to struggle when translating an idiom because of this. Experiments (Dankers et al., 2022) show that transformers (Vaswani et al., 2017) often fail to treat idioms in this manner and instead translate them compositionally resulting in poor translations.

This paper approaches the problem of clustering idioms in different languages based on their sense. Through this, we aim to improve semantic representations of idiomatic expressions to aid NLP tasks that rely on accurate sense disambiguation. In this paper, we make use of pre-trained cross-lingual language models (Conneau et al., 2020) to do this.

Our approach involves fine-tuning these models to generate cross-lingual vector representations of idioms based on sense. These representations can then be used to form sense clusters of idioms.

This idea can be further extended by leveraging idiom databases e.g. (Villavicencio et al., 2004) to identify the sense of an idiom not present in the database. By finding an idiom within the same cluster that is already in the database, we can infer the sense of the unknown idiom.

Idioms that share the same sense share a common meaning beyond their literal interpretations. Machine Translation systems often treat idioms compositionally and produce translations that are too literal and don't make sense in the translated text. The absence of parallel idiom datasets often hinders the effective training of transformers to address this challenge. We feel that our approach could aid this. Instead of training models to translate idioms in isolation which is often not practical, we propose a method capable of grouping idioms by their shared meaning. This enables the models to understand the meanings these idioms convey and the relationships between them across languages.

To evaluate our approach we conduct experiments using multi-lingual idiom datasets and assess the results.

2 Approach

In this paper, we employ BERT (Devlin et al., 2019) models that are pre-trained specifically for cross-lingual contexts to facilitate our approach. We fine-tune the model by training it on a dataset consisting of English idioms and corresponding German idioms. We developed a dataset of roughly 14,000 English and German Idioms for this purpose.

In order to train the model, we load the dataset and create *translation clusters* which consist of idioms that are direct translations of one another (taken from the website `dict.cc`). During training, we try to ensure the sense vectors of idioms in the same translation cluster are close to one another in order to create effective sense clusters.

We make use of the XLM-RoBERTa (Conneau et al., 2020) model which is trained on 2.5 terabytes of data in 100 different languages. XLM-RoBERTa

Proceedings of the First NLP4TIA Workshop, pages 13–19
Varna, Sep 8, 2023
https://doi.org/10.26615/978-954-452-091-5_003

Idiom	Gloss
es mit Fassung tragen	(to bear it with composure)
take it on the chin	
grin and bear it	
gute Miene zum bösen Spiel machen	(make a good face for the bad game)
in den sauren Apfel beißen	(bite into the sour apple)

Table 1: An example of a translation cluster. The gloss is provided for reference and is not part of the dataset.

Type	Count
English	6912
German	7763
Total	14675

Table 2: Dataset Statistics.

is trained with the multilingual MLM (Masked Language Model) objective. This allows the model to understand bi-directional context within text. This bi-directional context understanding is particularly crucial when dealing with idioms. XLM-RoBERTa produces contextual representations of the tokens that are passed to it. We then utilise pooling and an additional linear layer, to generate vector representations of the idioms.

We then employ a variety of clustering techniques to form sense-based clusters

2.1 Dataset

We hand-collected the dataset from the website `dict.cc`. We made use of a 90-5-5 train-test-validation split. Table 2 shows the composition of the dataset.

2.2 Model Architecture

The model architecture (Figure 1) consists of the XLM-RoBERTa model followed by a pooling layer and a linear layer which generates the phrase level embeddings. We made use of batch normalization (Ioffe and Szegedy, 2015) and weight decay (Loshchilov and Hutter, 2019) to make training more stable and reduce overfitting.

We investigate the effects of different pooling methods.

3 Training

3.1 Fine-Tuning

In order to train the model, we fine-tune the XLM-RoBERTa model and learn the weights for the final linear layer. We make use of the Adam optimizer (Kingma and Ba, 2017) during this process.

3.2 Triplet Loss

The triplet loss (Schroff et al., 2015) is defined as:

$$\mathcal{L} = \max(0, dist(a, p) - dist(a, n) + \alpha)$$

where:

- a is the anchor sample.
- p is a positive sample (same translation cluster as anchor).
- n is a negative sample (different translation cluster from anchor).
- $dist$ is the distance metric between samples.
- α is the margin that controls the minimum desired separation.

Triplet loss solely considers the distance between the anchor, positive and negative vectors. Some loss functions for the task of learning embeddings also consider the angle between the vectors (Wang et al., 2017). However, we felt that triplet loss worked well enough for our task.

4 Training Experiments

4.1 Embedding Dimensions

We investigated the effect of the number of nodes in the final linear layer (the number of dimensions of the sense embeddings that are produced) on training. As seen in Figure 2, the training is fairly similar for all of the embedding dimensions that we tested with the 64 and 128 dimensions performing the best. However, upon examining the validation losses, we found that the models with smaller embedding dimensions performed poorly. In our final model, we used an embedding size of 64.

4.2 Activation Functions

We also investigated the effects of different activation functions on the final linear layer. As seen in Figure 3, ELU, ReLU, Leaky ReLU and sigmoid

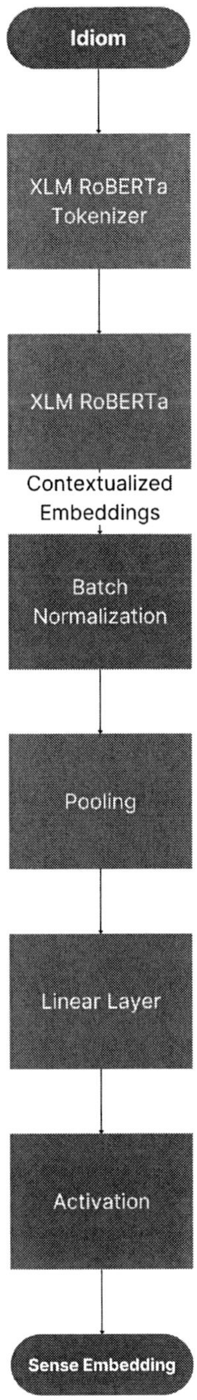

Figure 1: Model Architecture

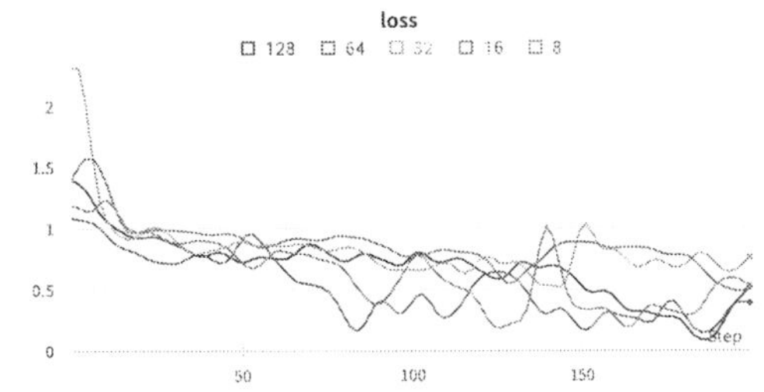

Figure 2: Loss (triplet) during training with different embedding dimensions.

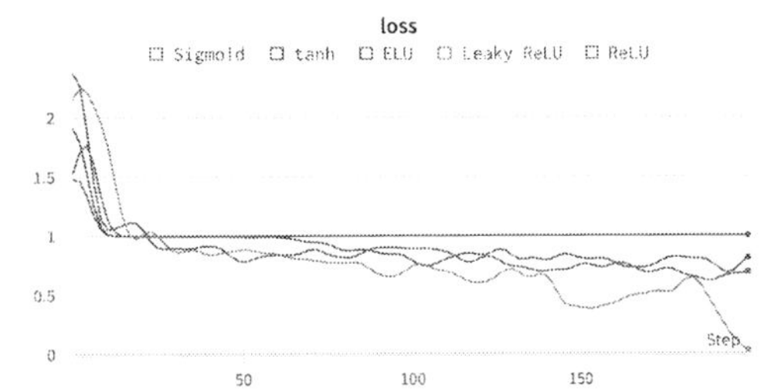

Figure 3: Loss (triplet) during training with different activation functions in the last layer.

all perform reasonably well with tanh performing poorly.

The reason for the poor performance could be due to the tendency of tanh to saturate hindering training.

We decided to use the Leaky ReLU activation function for our final model as it produced the most consistent results during the training process.

4.3 Learning Rate

After investigating the effect of the learning rate (Figure 4) on the training process, we found that a lower learning rate led to improved performance and convergence. For our final model, we used a learning rate of 0.00001.

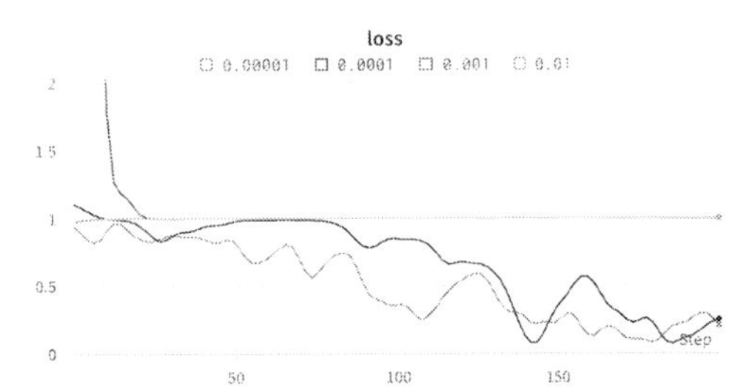

Figure 4: Loss (triplet) during training with different learning rates.

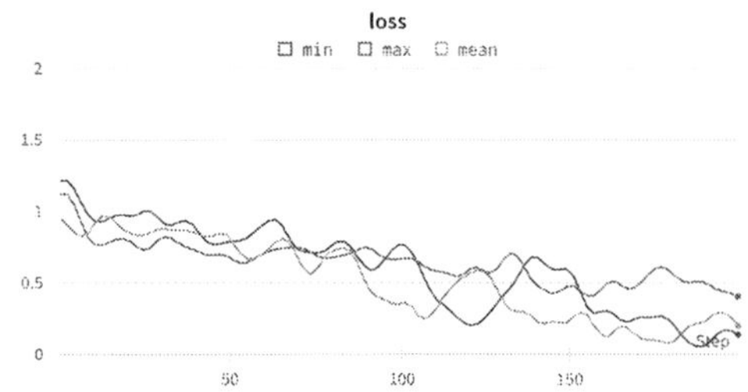

Figure 5: Loss (triplet) during training with different pooling methods.

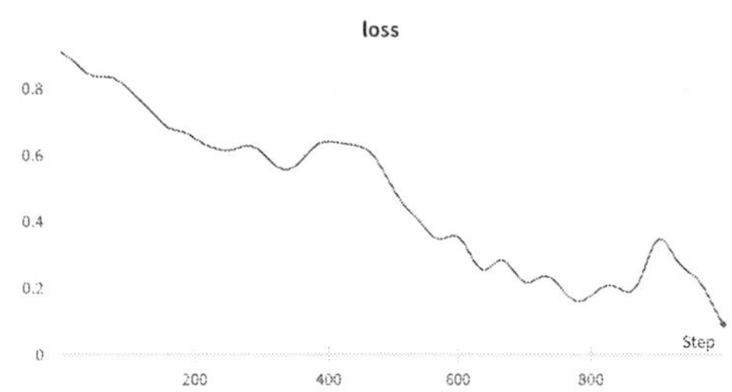

Figure 6: Loss during the training of the final model.

4.4 Pooling Method

Our investigations into the effects of different pooling methods on training (Figure 5) show that minimum pooling leads to the smallest loss. However, the validation losses for minimum pooling were inconsistent and mean pooling performed much better. For our final model, we used mean pooling.

4.5 Final Model Hyperparameters and Design Choices

Table 3 shows the design choices and hyperparameters of our final model. Figure 6 shows loss during the training of our final model.

Hyperparameter	**Value**
Batch Size	64
Weight Decay Rate	0.1
Learning Rate	0.00001
Embedding Dimensions	64
Linear Layer Activation	Leaky ReLU
Pooling Method	Mean
Training Epochs	1000

Table 3: Design choices and hyperparameters of our final model.

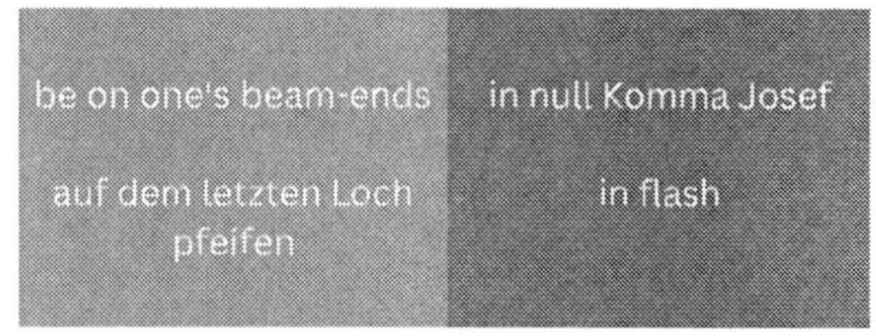

Figure 7: An extract from our clustering tests showing performance on clustering direct translations.

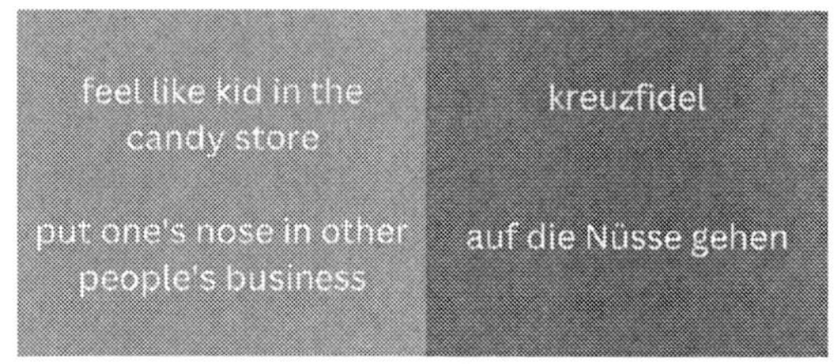

Figure 8: An extract from our clustering tests showing performance on clustering idioms of similar sense.

5 Clustering

We made use of the test data and applied various clustering algorithms to the encodings produced by the model. We made use of the K-means clustering, DBSCAN (Ester et al., 1996) and Bisecting K-Means (Steinbach et al., 2000) algorithms.

5.1 Direct Translations

We found that the model performed very well when attempting to cluster idioms that are direct translations of one another.

As seen in Figure 7, the model is able to effectively cluster idioms that are direct translations of one another.

5.2 Sense Clustering

Although the model is generally able to detect idioms with similar senses, it does struggle in some cases.

As seen in Figure 8, the model sometimes fails to properly cluster idioms of similar sense. 'kreuzfidel' (meaning to be as happy as a king) and 'feel like a kid in the candy store' both suggest a positive feeling and 'put one's nose in other people's business' and 'auf die Nüsse gehen' (meaning to get on someone's nerves) both have a negative sense. However, in this case, they were placed in different clusters.

We felt the failure was due to the choice of loss function. By using positive and negative samples, there is only a binary relationship between idioms.

This means the model fails to capture the nuanced similarities and differences between the idioms.

We also believe that the model weights relationships between idioms in the same language too heavily, which may hinder its ability to effectively cluster the idioms by their sense. This bias can result in clusters heavily dominated by a single language.

6 Model Evaluation

6.1 UMAP Projections

We utilised UMAP (McInnes et al., 2020) to project a subset of the sense vectors into 2 dimensions. This dimensionality reduction enables us to see more clearly the relationships the model is (and isn't) capturing.

Figure 9 shows the UMAP projection of the embeddings produced by the fine-tuned model and Figure 10 shows the UMAP projection of XLM-RoBERTa before the fine-tuning process. The idioms with the same colour in the graph are translations of one another so should be close together (if the model was trained effectively). The figures show that idioms that are translations of one another appear significantly closer to one another in the fine-tuned model. This indicates the model is capable of learning the semantic similarities between idioms in different languages as a result of the fine-tuning process.

6.2 Mean Reciprocal Rank

To assess the performance of the final model, we employed the Mean Reciprocal Rank (MRR) metric. We treated the sense embedding of a given idiom as a query and the sense embedding of the translation of that idiom as a target. We calculated MRR values on both the fine-tuned model and XLM-RoBERTa before fine-tuning so we could examine the effects of fine-tuning. By applying this technique, we aimed to gauge the model's effectiveness in placing idioms close to translations of themselves in a vector space. The results are shown in the Table 4.

From the data provided in the table, it's evident that the fine-tuning process had a significant positive impact on the model's performance. The MRR values for the fine-tuned model consistently outperformed those of the model without fine-tuning. This suggests that the fine-tuning process effectively enhanced the model's ability to generate sense-based vector representations of idioms.

Test No.	Batch Size	MRR before fine-tuning	MRR after fine-tuning
1	26	0.2184	0.4771
2	36	0.1205	0.3138
3	40	0.0698	0.1825

Table 4: The results of our MRR tests.

7 Conclusion and Future Work

In conclusion, our study presented a method of clustering idioms in different languages by their sense, making use of pre-trained transformer models. Our experiments show that our model works effectively but struggles in some circumstances.

During our tests, we found the model sometimes failed to cluster idioms of similar sense together. This can be partly attributed to the binary nature of triplet loss which fails to capture degrees of similarity between idioms.

Additionally, we identified a potential bias in the model's weighting of relationships between idioms in the same language.

To address these issues, further work can be done to mitigate these issues. We will work towards developing better loss functions and finding methods of reducing the bias.

Limitations

While our model shows promise at cross-lingual idiom sense clustering, we feel that there is room for improvement. This can partly be improved by larger datasets. By incorporating more diverse and comprehensive idiomatic expressions from different languages, the model can learn more robust representations and better capture the nuances of idiomatic senses.

Additionally, we believe that a more sophisticated loss function could further enhance the model's clustering capabilities. Instead of considering binary relationships between idioms, this loss function would consider the degree of relatedness between the idioms. This would allow the model to consider varying degrees of similarity between idioms resulting in better performance.

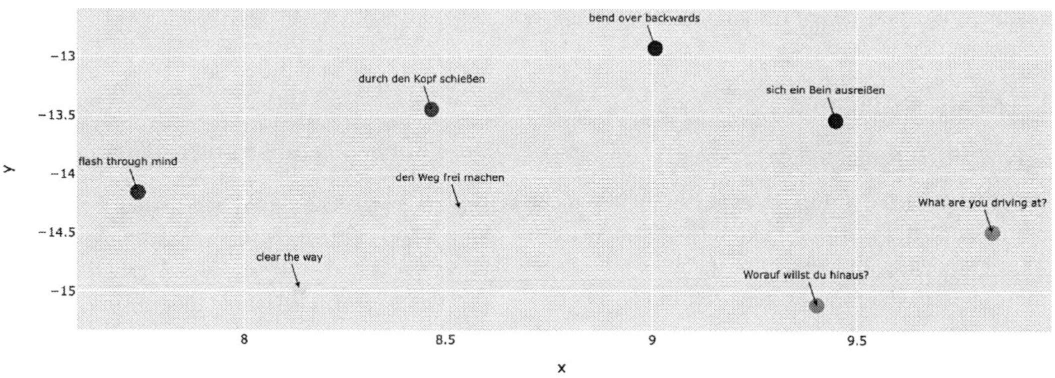

Figure 9: UMAP Projection of sense embeddings produced by the fine-tuned model.

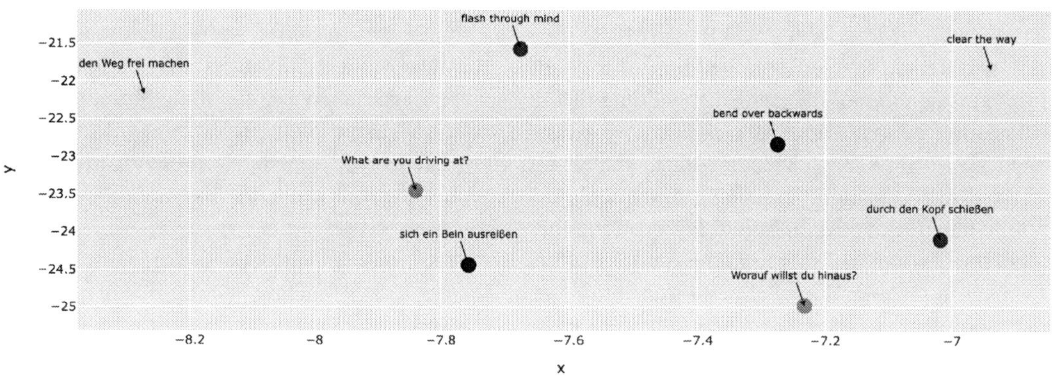

Figure 10: UMAP Projection of sense embeddings produced by XLM-RoBERTa before fine-tuning.

References

Alexis Conneau, Kartikay Khandelwal, Naman Goyal, Vishrav Chaudhary, Guillaume Wenzek, Francisco Guzmán, Edouard Grave, Myle Ott, Luke Zettlemoyer, and Veselin Stoyanov. 2020. Unsupervised cross-lingual representation learning at scale. In *Proceedings of the 58th Annual Meeting of the Association for Computational Linguistics*, pages 8440–8451, Online. Association for Computational Linguistics.

Verna Dankers, Christopher Lucas, and Ivan Titov. 2022. Can transformer be too compositional? analysing idiom processing in neural machine translation. In *Proceedings of the 60th Annual Meeting of the Association for Computational Linguistics (Volume 1: Long Papers)*, pages 3608–3626, Dublin, Ireland. Association for Computational Linguistics.

Jacob Devlin, Ming-Wei Chang, Kenton Lee, and Kristina Toutanova. 2019. Bert: Pre-training of deep bidirectional transformers for language understanding.

Martin Ester, Hans-Peter Kriegel, Jörg Sander, Xiaowei Xu, et al. 1996. A density-based algorithm for discovering clusters in large spatial databases with noise. In *kdd*, volume 96, pages 226–231.

Sergey Ioffe and Christian Szegedy. 2015. Batch normalization: Accelerating deep network training by reducing internal covariate shift. *CoRR*, abs/1502.03167.

Diederik P. Kingma and Jimmy Ba. 2017. Adam: A method for stochastic optimization.

Ilya Loshchilov and Frank Hutter. 2019. Decoupled weight decay regularization.

Leland McInnes, John Healy, and James Melville. 2020. Umap: Uniform manifold approximation and projection for dimension reduction.

Florian Schroff, Dmitry Kalenichenko, and James Philbin. 2015. IEEE. [link].

Michael Steinbach, George Karypis, and Vipin Kumar. 2000. A comparison of document clustering techniques.

Ashish Vaswani, Noam Shazeer, Niki Parmar, Jakob Uszkoreit, Llion Jones, Aidan N Gomez, Łukasz Kaiser, and Illia Polosukhin. 2017. Attention is all you need. *Advances in neural information processing systems*, 30.

Aline Villavicencio, Timothy Baldwin, and Benjamin Waldron. 2004. A multilingual database of idioms. In *LREC*.

Jian Wang, Feng Zhou, Shilei Wen, Xiao Liu, and Yuanqing Lin. 2017. Deep metric learning with angular loss.

Augmented Machine Translation Enabled by GPT4:

Performance Evaluation on Human-Machine Teaming Approaches

Ming Qian[1*], Huaqing Wu[2], Lenny Yang[2], Arthur Wan[3]

[1]PathFinders Translation and Interpretation Research, Cambridge, MA, USA
qianmi@pathfinders-transinterp.com
[2]American Translators Association (ATA) Certified Translator
michael@wutrans.com, lenny@y17inc.com
[3]Canadian Translators,Terminologists,Interpreters Council (CTTIC) Certified Translator
seertrans@gmail.com

Abstract

Translation has been modeled as a multiple-phase process where pre-editing analyses guide meaning transfer and interlingual restructure. Present-day machine translation (MT) tools provide no means for source text analyses. Generative AI with Large language modeling (LLM), equipped with prompt engineering and fine-tuning capabilities, can enable augmented MT solutions by explicitly including AI or human generated analyses/instruction, and/or human-generated reference translation as pre-editing or interactive inputs. Using an English-to-Chinese translation piece that had been carefully studied during a translator slam event, Fourt types of translation outputs on 20 text segments were evaluated: human-generated translation, Google Translate MT, instruction-augmented MT using GPT4-LLM, and Human-Machine-Teaming (HMT)-augmented translation based on both human reference translation and instruction using GPT4-LLM. While human translation had the best performance, both augmented MT approaches performed better than un-augmented MT. The HMT-augmented MT performed better than instruction-augmented MT because it combined the guidance and knowledge provided by both human reference translation and style instruction. However, since it is unrealistic to generate sentence-by-sentence human translation as MT input, better approaches to HMT-augmented MT need to be invented. The evaluation showed that generative AI with LLM can enable new MT workflow facilitating pre-editing analyses and interactive restructuring and achieving better performance.

1 Introduction

The core of machine translation (MT) is the automation of the full translation process (Hutchins 2009). The degree of MT automation can vary: fully automatic machine translation, human-aided machine translation, or machine-aided human translation (Sager 1994). Nearly all MT systems currently in use rely on the assistance of human operators. Human involvement can come in three different modes: (1) pre-editing the source text, (2) interaction between system and human operator, or (3) post-editing. The dominant MT work model at present days is to use human translators as post-editors (correction/revision) on MT output. Dominant MT tools (e.g., Google Translate, Bing Microsoft Translator, or DeepL) convert text from a source language into an equivalent passage in the target language, but they do not provide any pre-editing analysis results as

Proceedings of the First NLP4TIA Workshop, pages 20–31
Varna, Sep 8, 2023
https://doi.org/10.26615/978-954-452-091-5_004

guiding instructions or any interaction mechanisms between the human and MT system.

Translation has been modeled as a multiple-phase process where pre-editing analyses guide meaning transfer and interlingual restructure. There are many differing theories that conceptualize different phases of the translation process.

Nida's translation theory of dynamic equivalence (Nida 1964, 1974, 2006; Kim 2015) divides the translation process into three phases (illustrated in Figure): (1) analysis (based on the source language characteristics), (2) transfer (between the source and target language), and (3) restructuring (based on the target language characteristics). The analysis phase reflects the understanding and interpretation that can be used to guide the transfer and restructuring phases.

Present-day MT tools do not provide explicit

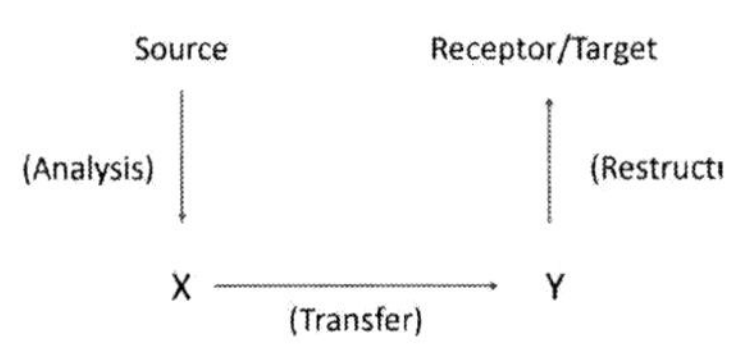

Figure 1: Nida's translation model with multiple phases: analysis, transfer, and restructuring.

means for users to analyze the source language, which would then be used to guide the transferring and restructuring process.

Another translation process model (Pym, 2011) also has three phases: (1) recognize the problem (how to say X in target language?), (2) generate many alternative solutions, (3) select one solution (out of many).

Present-day MT tools do not provide explicit alternative solutions and let users select a solution; nor do they provide explanations as to why the final output it provides is more accurate than the alternatives.

(Austermuhl, 2001) pointed out that a transfer architecture for MT included three separate stages: (1) analysis, (2) transfer, (3) synthesis/generation. In addition, it stated that pre-editing and interaction with the MT system before and during the MT process could be strategies to improve MT quality outside of post-editing.

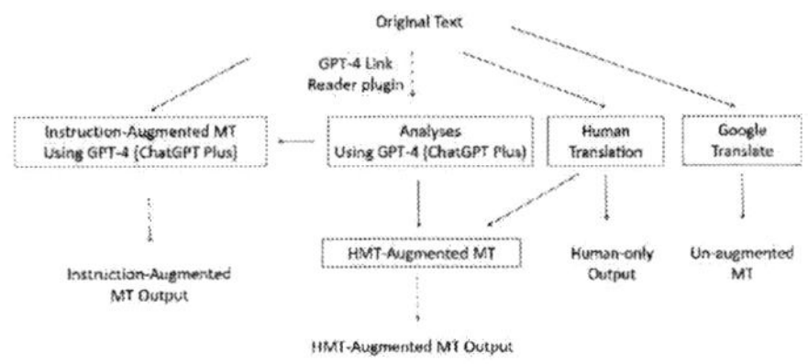

Figure 2: The story was translated by a human translator, Google Translate (un-augmented MT), instruction-augmented, and HMT-augmented MT using LLM-GPT4.

Present-day MT tools do not provide mechanisms for pre-editing and human-machine interaction during the MT process.

In (Carl, 2011), the human translation process was studied using eye tracking. In the end, three phases were identified: (1) preparation phase during which initial document reading was performed and translation strategy was chosen. (2) drafting phase. (3) revision phase. Furthermore, different translators were found to have different styles: large versus small context planners (who read more or less content before they made strategy choices or started to translate), backtracker versus non-backtrackers (who did or did not frequently go back to revise), and various orientation styles: systematic, skimming, or head start without orientation.

Present-day MT tools do not provide mechanisms to support these translation style variations.

Following the post-editing only work model, since human experts cannot provide pre-editing and interactive guidance to MT system through the many mechanisms described above, achieving high-quality translations is challenging and time-consuming, leading to inaccurate or unnatural results.

The solution to the aforementioned limiting factors could come in the form of Generative Large Language Models (LLM) such as GPT4, which could be the game changer that enables all or most mechanisms described above (Table 1).

GPT models can achieve very competitive high-quality translations for high resource languages, even though they were not originally designed to be used as MT tools. One of the unique features of GPT models is the prompting engineering (Zhou, 2022), where precise and context-specific instructions or queries—known as prompts—can be crafted to elicit desired responses from language models. Prompts guide the model and help shape its behavior and output. In this study, we focus on evaluating the approach to provide pre-editing or interactive guidance to MT using prompting engineering.

Unlike "traditional" MT tools, GPT4 based augmented MT can fully reflect pre-editing preparation, recognition, analyses, and human-machine interaction by explicitly including AI and human-generated text analyses and human-generated guidance or translation in the prompt.

Phases of Translation process models	Generative AI LLM features supporting pre-editing and human-machine interaction
Pre-editing → Interaction →Post-editing (Sager 1994) Analysis →Transfer →Restructure (Nida 1964, 1974, 2006; Kim 2015) Recognition→Generation →Selection (Pym 2011) Analysis→Transfer →Synthesis/Generation (Austermuhl, 2001) Preparation →Drafting →Revision (Carl 2011)	- Prompting engineering (e.g. OpenAI/GPT or Google Bard) can represent analysis results, transfer guidelines/strategies using instructions and few-shot examples. - Multiple drafts that are distinct from each other can be generated to support multi-version selection and HMT (e.g., Google BARD alternative drafts feature). - LLM-based Chatbox (e.g. OpenAI/BARD) enables human-machine interaction. - Larger and complex context can be addressed through LLM finetuning. - ...

Table 1: Phases in different translation process models can be implemented through pre-editing and interactive components that can be enabled by various features of generative AI LLMs.

Using an English-to-Chinese translation piece that had been carefully analyzed and discussed during a translator slam event, a Human-generated Chinese translation of an English story (`https://www.thecut.com/2020/03/book-excerpt-samantha-irbys-wow-no-thank-you.html`) was compared with multiple Chinese translations generated using GPT4 and related plugin software (illustrated in Figure) following the steps below:

1) Writing styles of the original English story were analyzed using GPT4 (ChatGPT Plus) and a GPT4 plugin (ChatGPT Plus Link Reader).
2) The story was translated from English to Chinese with the additional writing style instructions (derived in step 1) using GPT4 (ChatGPT Plus). This MT version was named as the instruction-augmented MT.
3) The story was translated from English to Chinese using both human-generated translation (as a reference translation) and using the additional writing style instructions (derived in step 1) in the prompt text using GPT4 (ChatGPT Plus). This MT version was named as the human-machine teaming (HMT) augmented MT.

Using 20 translation instances, two human translators assessed the pros and cons of the two augmented MT approaches using GPT4 over human-generated translation and an un-augmented MT using Google Translate.

2 Human Translation Slam Event

Translation slam events have been organized by the American Translators Associations (ATA) to have two translators go head-to-head to display their works on the same translation source text so the two translators have an opportunity to glimpse each other's work on the same content. Audiences can also hear their discussions and comments during the event.

In June 2023, an English-to-Chinese Translation Slam was hosted by ATA's Chinese Language Division (CLD) featuring two professional translators: Sijin Xian and Arthur Wan. They competed to translate a challenging English text into Chinese and compare notes on their techniques and choices during the discussion session (see the original English text and a compilation of the two translations in the appendix). Their comments on each other's work were recorded to discover how each translator analyzes, translates, and revises their translations. Based on the detailed discussion during the slam event, Sijin's translation focused

User (Prompt)
Please read the story at **https://www.thecut.com/2020/03/book-excerpt-samantha-irbys-wow-no-thank-you.html** and make a list of the author's writing style.
ChatGPT (Used Link Reader)
Based on the excerpt from Samantha Irby's essay collection "Wow, No Thank You.", here are some characteristics of her writing style:

1. Humorous and Self-deprecating: Irby often uses humor and self-deprecation to engage her readers. She makes fun of herself and her situations, which adds a light-hearted tone.
2. Conversational Tone: Her writing style is very conversational, feeling personal and relatable.
3. **Vivid Descriptions**: Irby uses vivid and detailed descriptions to paint a clear picture of her experiences. This helps to immerse the reader in her stories.
4. **Casual Language and Slang**: She uses casual language, slang, and colloquialisms, which contributes to the conversational and informal tone of her writing.
5. Honesty and Authenticity: Irby's writing is characterized by its honesty and authenticity. She doesn't shy away from discussing personal and sometimes uncomfortable topics.
6. Anecdotes: She uses anecdotes to illustrate points and make writing more relatable.
7. **Exaggeration for Effect**: Irby often uses exaggeration to emphasize her points.
8. Direct Address: She frequently addresses the reader directly, which helps to establish a connection between her and the reader.
9. Use of Rhetorical Questions: Irby often uses rhetorical questions to engage the reader and encourage them to think more deeply about the topics she's discussing.
10. Pop Culture References: She incorporates pop culture references into her writing, which can make her work feel more current and relatable to a wide audience.

Table 2: writing style analysis report generated by GPT4 Link Reader plug-in. The bolded entries are styles that were identified by both humans and GPT4 Link Reader plug-in.

The prompt for instruction-augmented MT	The prompt for HMT-augmented MT
Translate the following sentences to Chinese reflecting the following writing styles (if applicable): humorous, self-deprecating, conversational tone, vivid description, casual language and slang, honesty and authenticity, use of anecdotes, exaggeration for effect, direct address, use of rhetorical questions, and pop culture reference. Original English: ... The full translation to Chinese is: ... (GPT4 output)	Revise the following Chinese translation reflecting the following writing styles (if applicable): humorous and self-deprecating, conversational tone, vivid description, casual language and slang, honesty and authenticity, Original English: ... Chinese translation (by the human translator) is: ... The Revised Chinese translation is: ... (GPT4 output)

Table 3: Prompts for instruction-augmented and HMT-augmented MT using GPT4.

more on style transfer between languages while Arthur's translation focused more on word selection. We selected Sijin's version to represent human translation because the augmented MTs also orient towards style transfer through instruction and human inputs.

3 Writing style analysis by human experts and GPT4

During the translation slam event, the two human translators discussed the writing style of the English writer and their approaches to reflect related styles in their Chinese translations. In addition, ChatGPT plus's Link Reader plugin was used in the prompt text to generate a style analysis report for the original English story.

3.1 Writing styles recognized by human experts

During the slam event, the two human translators recognized the following writing style elements in the English version of the original story:

(1) Confessional writing style: more focus on shocking or even irritating the reader instead of presenting the facts objectively.
(2) Informal colloquialisms, not afraid of using dirty words to express emotion.
(3) Well-selected specific subtle details that trigger sympathetic responses from readers.
(4) Reflective of the unique personality of the author (e.g., focus and amplify on small details).
(5) The author also had worked as a professional narrator before; therefore, the conversational style is unique: with fast paced talking firing off phrases like a "machine gun".
(6) ...

3.2 Writing styles recognized by GPT4

ChatGPT Plus' Link Reader plugin was used to generate a style analysis report on the story (Table 2). It can be seen that the styles detected by LLM-GPT4 included many entries that were detected by human translators as well: casual language and slang versus informal colloquialisms, vivid description versus unique effects achieved by well-selected subtle words/phrases, exaggeration for effect versus confessional writing style. The GPT4-generated report also includes several other writing styles that were not mentioned by human translators.

4 Comparison of Human Translation, Google Translate MT, Instruction-Augmented MT and HMT-Augmented MT

The purpose of this section is to compare translation results generated by:

(1) MT by Google Translate.
(2) a human translator.
(3) instruction-augmented MT using LLM-GPT4 prompt with style instruction.
(4) HMT-augmented MT using LLM-GPT4 prompts with style instruction and human-generated reference translation.

The discussion by the two human professional translators during the translation slam event indicated that while one of them focused more on style transfer between languages, the other focused more on word choice. The translation produced by the translator who had focused more on style transfer is chosen to represent human translation as described in (2) and to serve as the human-generated reference translation as described in (4).

4.1 Prompts for augmented MT using GPT4

Table 3 lists the two prompts for augmented MT.

4.2 Evaluator qualifications and guidelines

Two evaluators were selected to evaluate the four versions of translation. Both evaluators are American Translators Association (ATA) certified translators who are native Chinese speakers, have 15-20 years of experience, hold translation degrees, and have worked on a wide variety of text types in the language pair. Detailed qualifications of the two evaluators can be found at `http://www.wutrans.com/` and `www.y17.us`.

The evaluators were instructed to rate translation output using a 5-point Likert scale score: very satisfied (2), somewhat satisfied (1), neither satisfied nor dissatisfied (0), somewhat dissatisfied (-1), and very dissatisfied (-2). The evaluators were encouraged to provide the reasons for the ratings they gave.

Figure shows the rating scores given by the two evaluators using color scales. Human translation had the best performance based on evaluations. Conversely, GPT4 augmented translations using either style instruction or human input in the prompt performed better than MT without augmentation using Google

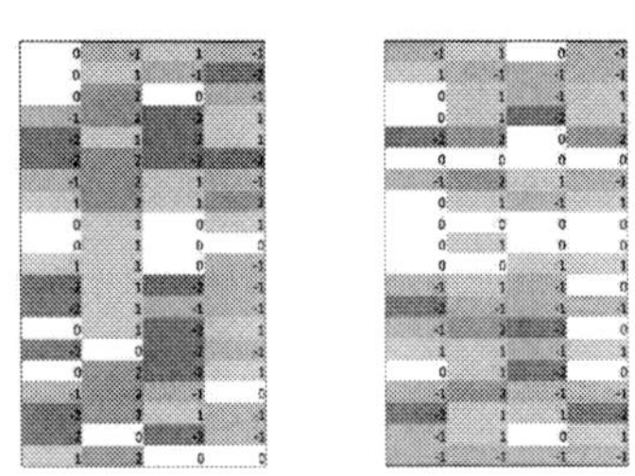

Figure 3: Color scaled rating scores by the two evaluators (4 columns are for Google Translate, human, instruction-augmented and HMT-augmented MT).

Translate. HMT-augmented MT performed better than instruction -augmented MT because it combined the guidance and knowledge provided by both human reference translation and style instruction.

Tables 4, 5, 6, and 7 show the ratings and the summarized reasons provided by the evaluators.

Table 4 shows the ratings and summarized reasons towards MT (Google Translate) results for all 20 instances. The main criticism was that MT did a lot direct (literal) translation, which led to mistranslation and awkwardness in the target language result.

Table shows the ratings and summarized reasons towards human translator results for all 20 instances. The main compliment was that the human translator uses more free translations to focus on conveying intended tone and meaning in target language.

Table shows the ratings and summarized reasons towards instruction-augmented MT (using LLM-GPT4) results for all 20 instances. The main criticism is on mistranslation and unnatural expressions.

Table shows the ratings and summarized reasons towards HMT-augmented MT (using LLM-GPT4) results for all 20 instances. The main criticism is still on mistranslation and unnatural expressions, but HMT-augmented MT demonstrates better performance than instruction -augmented MT because it has human-generated reference translation as an input. Therefore, in some instances, satisfactory free translations were generated.

Instances	Evaluators' ratings and reasons
1	(-1) direct translation does not sound natural to native ears. (0) N/A
2	(1) direct translation maintains the meaning. (0) N/A
3	(1) direct translation lacks intended tone the author aimed to convey. (0) N/A
4	(0) direct translation maintains the meaning (-1) N/A
5	(-2) incorrect translation (-2) wrong translation
6	(0) N/A (-2) wrong translation
7	(-1) direct translation lacks the intended tone in the original (-1) wrong target word selected
8 - 11	(0) N/A (1) N/A
12	(-1) incorrect translation; does not flow well (-2) Some words are mistranslated
13	(-2) incorrect translation (-2) incorrect translation
14	(-1) incorrect translation (0) N/A
15	(1) N/A (-2) wrong translation
16	(0) N/A (0) N/A
17	(-1) incorrect translation (-1) misleading
18	(-2) incorrect translation (-2) mistranslation
19	(-1) does not sound natural (-2) mistranslate multiple words
20	(-1) direct translation but incorrect meaning (1) N/A

Table 4: Ratings and summarized reasons on MT results (N/A: no reason provided).

Instances	Evaluators' ratings and reasons
1	(1) N/A (-1) wrong register level
2	(-1) incoherent meaning (1) N/A
3	(1) free translation captures the intended tone (2) N/A
4	(1) free translation captures the intended tone (2) N/A
5	(2) free translation captures the intended tone (1) Good translation with the sentences re-organized
6	(0) N/A (2) Good translation. Exactly what means.
7	(2) free translation captures the intended tone (2) Good translation. Exactly what it means.
8	(1) N/A (2) Good word choice
9	(0) N/A (1) N/A
10	(1) free translation captures the intended tone (1) free translation selects a word that is different from the source, but is a smooth word that can be used here
11	(0) N/A (1) N/A
12	(1) free translation captures the intended tone (1) N/A
13-16	(-1) N/A (1) N/A
17	(2) free translation is appealing (2) N/A
18	(1) free translation is appealing (2) reflects true meaning and adopt a source word seamless into the target
19	(1) free translation is simplified and appealing (0) N/A
20	(-1) direct translation but incorrect (2) smoother than other translations

Table 5: Ratings and summarized reasons on human results (N/A: no reason provided).

Instances	Evaluators' ratings and reasons
1	(0) direct translation but not appealing to readers (1) N/A
2	(-1) incoherent meaning (-1) awkward expression, not natural
3	(-1) not natural (0) N/A
4	(-2) direct translation sounds awful (-2) does not make sense
5	(0) OK can be better (-2) wrong translation
6	(0) N/A (-2) wrong translation
7 -11	(1) N/A (1) N/A
12	(-1) incorrect translation and does not flow well (-2) some phrases were translated incorrectly
13	(-1) N/A (-1) a phrase was translated wrong
14	(-2) incorrect translation (-2) incorrect translation
15	(-1) N/A (-2) wrong translation
16	(-2) wrong translation (-2) wrong translation
17	(-1) wrong translation (-1) misleading translation
18	(1) free translation and correct (1) correctly express the meaning of the source text
19	(0) N/A (-2) several mistranslated words
20	(-1) direct translation but wrong (0) N/A

Table 6: Ratings and summarized reasons on instruction-augmented results (N/A: no reason provided).

5 Conclusion

Generative AI with Large language modeling (LLM), equipped with prompt engineering and fine-tuning capabilities, can enable augmented MT solutions by explicitly including AI or human generated analyses, and/or human-generated reference translation as pre-editing or interactive inputs.

Using the English-to-Chinese translation piece, we evaluated translation outputs on 20 text segments using human-generated translation,

Instances	Evaluators' ratings and reasons
1	(-1) direct translation, not natural (-1) misinterpret the circumstance
2	(-1) incoherent meaning (-2) "invent meaning" that does not exist in the source
3	(1) free translation captures the original tone (-1) too much transcreation
4	(1) free translation captures the right tone (1) N/A
5	(2) free translation captures the original tone (1) Good sentence reorganization
6	(0) N/A (-2) wrong translation
7	(-1) N/A (-1) mistranslation (general versus specific)
8	(1) N/A (2) N/A
9	(0) N/A (-1) register level (too strong a word is used)
10	(0) N/A (0) N/A
11	(1) N/A (-1) register level (formal versus casual)
12	(0) N/A (-1) some mistranslated words
13-16	(-1) N/A (-1) a chosen target word does not make sense
14	(0) N/A (1) N/A
15	(1) N/A (-2) wrong translation
16	(0) N/A (1) N/A
17	(-1) wrong translation (0) not clear
18	(-2) wrong translation (-1) literal translation does not make sense
19	(1) free translation that is appealing (-1) missing connective word
20	(-1) not natural (0) N/A

Table 7: Ratings and summarized reasons on HMT-augmented results (N/A: no reason provided).

Google Translate MT, instruction-augmented MT using GPT4-LLM, and Human-Machine-Teaming (HMT) augmented translation based on both human reference translation and style instruction using GPT4-LLM.

The evaluation results show that while human translation had the best performance, both augmented MT approaches performed better than MT without augmentation. The HMT-augmented MT performed better than instruction-augmented MT because it combined the guidance and knowledge from both human reference translation and AI-generated style instruction. However, since it is unrealistic to generate sentence-by-sentence human translation as input to MT, better approaches to HMT-augmented MT need to be studied further. The evaluation showed that generative AI with LLM can enable new MT workflow facilitating pre-editing analyses and interactive restructuring and achieving better performance.

Acknowledgments

We wish to extend our gratitude to Sijin Xian and Rony Gao for their dedication in orchestrating the translation slam event, generating, and curating the translation data for this manuscript.

References

Austermuhl, Frank, 2001. Electronic tools for translators. Routledge.

Carl, Michael, Dragsted, B. and Jakobsen, A.L., 2011. On the systematicity of human translation processes. Session 2-Translation as a profession. Tralogy I. Métiers et technologies de la traduction: quelles convergences pour l'avenir?, p.10p.

ChatGPT Extension, 2023, Exploring the Capabilities of Link Reader ChatGPT Plugin, available at: `https://chatonai.org/link-reader-chatgpt-plugin` (accessed: August 25th, 2023).

Hutchins, W.J. and Somers, H.L., 2009. An introduction to machine translation.

Kim, Dohun, 2015. Dynamic Equivalence: Nida's Perspective and Beyond. Skase Journal of Translation and Interpretation, 8(1), pp.60-75.

Nida, Eugene A., 1964. Toward a science of translating: with special reference to principles and procedures involved in Bible translating. Brill Archive.

Nida, Eugene A. and Taber, C.R. eds., 1974. The theory and practice of translation (Vol. 8). Brill Archive. Ashok K. Chandra, Dexter C. Kozen, and Larry J. Stockmeyer. 1981. Alternation. Journal of the Association for Computing Machinery, 28(1):114-133.

Nida, Eugene A., 2006. Theories of translation, (4), pp.11-14.

Pym, Anthony, 2011. What technology does to translating. Translation&Interpreting, 3(1), pp.1-9.

Sager, Juan C., 1994. Language engineering and translation: Consequences of automation (Vol. 1). John Benjamins Publishing.

Zhou, Y., Muresanu, A.I., Han, Z., Paster, K., Pitis, S., Chan, H. and Ba, J., 2022. Large language models are human-level prompt engineers. arXiv preprint arXiv:2211.01910.

Appendix

A segment-by-segment compilation of the two translations together with the source text

Source (English)	Translation Version 1 (by Sijin Xian)	Translation Version 2 (by Arthur Wan)
The Worst Friend Date I Ever Had	我的“社死”之交	我经历的最糟的朋友会面
An excerpt from Samantha Irby's new essay collection Wow, No Thank You.	节选自萨曼莎·尔比全新散文集《哇，不了谢谢》	节选自萨曼莎-艾比的新散文集《哇，不用了，谢谢》。
By Samantha Irby	作者：萨曼莎·尔比	作者：萨曼莎-艾比
https://www.thecut.com/2020/03/book-excerpt-samantha-irbys-wow-no-thank-you.html	https://www.thecut.com/2020/03/book-excerpt-samantha-irbys-wow-no-thank-you.html	https://www.thecut.com/2020/03/book-excerpt-samantha-irbys-wow-no-thank-you.html
You don't have to cry for me, but listen: trying to make new friends as an adult is the hardest thing I have ever attempted. Harder than multiple colonoscopies? Yes. Harder than listening to the dentist pry my tooth bone away from my jawbone while I lie there wide awake? Also yes!	同情的眼泪倒犯不着，就听我说一句：设法在成年人的世界里结交新朋友，是我努力做过的最艰难的事。有比做好几次肠镜还艰难吗？有。有比躺在牙医椅上，眼睁睁地听着我的牙骨从我的下巴骨上被撬走还艰难吗？也有！	你不必为我伤心，但听着：作为一个成年人，尝试结交新朋友是我所尝试过所有事情中最痛苦的。比多次结肠镜检查还痛苦？是的。比我醒着躺在那里听牙医将我的牙骨从下颚骨上撬下来还痛苦？答案也是肯定的！
When I moved to Kalamazoo from Chicago, I thought for sure that I was going to be happy staying at home and never going outside. And, for the most part, I am. I get to travel and work in fancy cities with mass transit and Ethiopian food, then come back and pay $1.87 for a gallon of gas for the car that I can park anywhere on my sprawling 2,000 acres of land that were practically free. Okay, I'm exaggerating, but my point is FUCK THE CITY.	我从芝加哥搬来卡拉马祖的时候，心想我肯定可以惬意地宅在家里，门都不用出。结果，我大体上是挺满足的。我可以趁着去外地工作，领略有发达的公共交通和埃塞俄比亚菜的华丽都市，然后回来付个一加仑只要 1 刀 8 毛 7 的油钱，把车随便停在我家几乎白送的 2000 英亩的辽阔土地上。好吧，这话夸张了，但我的重点是：去他妈的大城市！	当我从芝加哥搬到卡拉马祖时，我确信我将会快乐地呆在家里，再不出门。而且，在大多数情况下，我就是如此。我可以在有公共交通和埃塞俄比亚食物的光鲜城市旅行和工作，然后回来给我的汽车加 1.87 美元一加仑的汽油，在我那 2000 英亩的近乎免费的广袤土地上，我可以随意停车。好吧，我是在夸大其词，但我的意思是：去他妈的城市！

But, how does one make friends without an office to go to? Or a club to participate in? Or various PTA meetings to grimace at each other through? Are you just supposed to walk up to an interesting-looking person on the street and ask them to be your friend? I don't know if this is some kind of reverse profiling, but I can usually glance at a person and know at first sight that we're probably going to get along. I don't have it down to a science (I'm not researching shit, dude), but here are some dead giveaways: they have interesting, alternative, "cool person" hair, dumb tattoos, or are carrying a book, multiplied by a factor of ten if it happens to be one I wrote (I'm sorry — I am an egomaniac).

可是，一个人在这种情况下要上哪儿交朋友呢？我一不在办公室上班，二不参加俱乐部，三不去各种家委会上和人挤眉弄眼暗送嘲讽。我难不成要在大街上直接走到一个貌似有趣的人跟前，让人家当我朋友？不知道这是不是一种褒义的以貌取人，反正我通常扫一眼就立马能知道我和一个人大概会合得来。我倒没得出什么科学体系（大哥，我才不会费这破劲儿去做研究呢），但吃准了几点特征：这人通常有别致、另类、酷范儿十足的发型，傻里傻气的纹身，或是拿着一本书——要是还刚好是我写的，就十倍加分（不好意思啊，我是个自大狂）。

但是，一个人如果不去办公室，又怎么交友呢？如果不去俱乐部呢？如果也不去各种家长教师联谊会的会议上互相挤眉弄眼呢？难道你就指望在大街上走到一个看起来很有趣的人面前，要求其成为你的朋友？我不知道这是否是某种逆向分析，但我通常可以瞥见一个人后，第一眼就知道我们可能会相处得很好。我没把它归结为一门科学（哥们，我不是在做什么狗屁研究），但这里有某种致命信号：这人有趣的、另类的、"酷哥/靓妹"的头发，帅气的纹身，或者拿本书，如果它碰巧是我写的，那就要更好十倍（对不起——我是个自大狂。

Have you ever considered what a friendship is, or what any of your current friendships are, and thought about how to present that to a prospective new friend? You know, like how you are going to eventually be sending them selfies of you trying on 12 similar-yet-slightly-different pairs of glasses in your ophthalmologist's waiting room while your garbage insurance is being processed? How do you convince a stranger to give you their real email when you are going to litter their gmail.com

你有没有思考过友情是什么，或者你目前的友谊都是些什么情况？你有没有想过要怎么把这些向你的求友对象交代？你懂的，比如你怎么跟人说，等你们混熟了，你会在眼科医生的等候室里一边等你那垃圾保险走程序，一边发你试戴 12 副大同小异的眼镜的自拍？既然你明明会往人家的 Gmail 邮箱乱塞没头没脑的废话，那还怎么说服一个陌生人把真正的邮箱地址给你？

你有没有想过什么是友谊？或者你目前的朋友是怎样的？并考虑如何向潜在的新朋友呈现这些？就像你最终要给他们发送你在眼科医生等候室里试戴 12 副相似又略不同的眼镜的自拍照时你的垃圾保险正在处理中那样吗？你如何说服一个你肯定会在其 Gmail.com 上胡说八道留言的陌生人、让他给你真的电子邮件呢？

with dumb nonsense?		
A few years ago (before I moved to Michigan and joined my wife's community of backyard composters and travel-soccer chauffeurs), my lady and I went to her friend's costume wedding and — I know you already know this, but let me just say it for anyone who is new or still has a shred of hopefulness in their heart — I did not wear a costume.	几年前，我和我老婆去了她一个朋友的婚礼。（那时我还没有追随我家夫人搬来密歇根州，加入她那在后院堆肥和开车接送孩子去各地踢足球的圈子。）婚礼是变装主题的——我知道你已经有数了，但容我对新来的或心里还存有一丝希望的读者说：我并没有扮角色。我上一次万圣节变装，还是在 1986 年林肯小学的二年级变装游行上（不免俗地喊个口号：海豚队加油）。那时我唯一能想到的装扮就是"家庭主妇"，虽然对这个概念一知半解，但我想着穿上我妈破得抽条的旧袍子，	几年前（在我搬到密歇根并加入我妻子的后院堆肥者和旅行足球司机圈子之前），我娘子和我去参加她朋友的礼服婚礼，然而——我知道你懂的，但让我告诉新来的或心中尚有一丝希望的人——我没穿礼服。我最后一次穿万圣节服装是 1986 年在林肯小学二年级的服装游行中（加油，海豚），我唯一能想到的服装是 "家庭主妇" ——一个我那时还不能充分理解的概念，但我认为我可以用我妈妈的破旧长袍、半融化的锅铲和她在新压卷发后的晚上睡觉用过的缎面帽子来扮个大概
The last time I wore a Halloween costume was in the second-grade costume parade at Lincoln Elementary School in 1986 (go, dolphins), and the only costume I could come up with was "housewife," a concept I didn't fully understand but thought I could approximate with my mom's tattered old robe, a half-melted spatula, and the satin cap she slept in the nights after a fresh press 'n' curl. Because I was a Very Large Son, everyone just thought I had worn my shitty pajamas to school.	拿上一个一半已经熔化了的铲子，再来一顶她把头发拉直烫卷后的头几天晚上会戴着睡觉的缎面帽，就八九不离十了。由于我的"大块头儿子"形象，大家只是以为我穿着烂不啦叽的睡衣去了学校。	。因为我是个特大号儿子，所以大家都以为我穿着我的烂睡衣去了学校。
Anyway, my wife and I were at this wedding where I knew a few people well enough to say "Hi" but not well enough to say "Hi, ______," and as we're sitting in our assigned dinner seats I'm looking around the room, taking it all in, wondering who I can latch on to in the hopes of a semipermanent relationship once I officially moved to Kalamazoo. A dude named Ike	再扯回婚礼的事。现场我认识的人不多，而且只熟到能说声"嗨"，还没熟到能叫出"嗨，某某某"来。我们在晚宴的指定座位坐下后，我环顾房间，消化着眼前的一切，寻思着可以"勾搭"上谁，好在正式搬来卡拉马祖之后发展一段还算地久天长的友谊。自助餐还没准备就绪，不夸张地说，我完全是奔着这	总之，我和我妻子参加了这个婚礼，我认识那儿的几个人，可以跟他们打招呼说"你好"，但还没熟到说"xx，你好"的程度。当我们坐在指定的晚餐座位上时，我环顾房间，一切尽收眼底，脑子里想着一旦我正式搬到卡拉马祖，我可以抓住谁才能建立半永久的关系。在我们等待自助餐的时候

came and sat next to me as we waited for the buffet to be set up, literally the only reason I braved a room full of people unironically dressed as Tolkien characters. He was wearing a Scientology uniform as his costume, and I immediately fell deeply in love. I talked to Ike for a while, writing his name in permanent marker on the Potential New Friends list in my mind.	顿饭，才硬着头皮直面这一屋子正儿八经打扮成托尔金笔下的魔幻角色的人。等待时，一个叫艾克的哥们儿过来坐在了我旁边，他一身科学教徒制服的扮相，让我一见倾心。我和他聊了一会儿，用永久性记号笔在心里的新朋友备选名单上写下他的名字。	，一个叫艾克(Ike）的老兄走过来坐在我旁边，这简直就是我面对一屋子人不伦不类地打扮成托尔金怪人的唯一原因。他穿着科学教的制服作为服装道具，我立刻深深爱上了他。我和艾克聊了一会儿，把他的名字用永久标记写在我心中的潜在新朋友名单上。
After he abandoned me to go fill up his plate with communal vegan enchiladas from the hot bar, a cool-looking woman with shiny bangs and interesting glasses (PRO) carrying a tiny crying baby (CON) and wearing a Ruth Bader Ginsburg costume (NEUTRAL) came over to introduce herself to me. We got on like a house on fire. After a few minutes, my palms started to sweat in anticipation of what would surely be an awkward transition from a pleasant introductory conversation to the method by which I could secure her contact information to lock down a future friendship.	后来他抛下我，端着盘子到热食区去狂拿公共的纯素焗墨西哥卷饼去了。这时，一个酷炫女人走过来向我介绍了自己。她有闪亮的刘海和别致的眼镜（加分），抱着一个哭嚎的小婴儿（扣分），一副大法官露丝·贝德·金斯伯格的装扮（不加不扣）。我们一见如故，打得火热。几分钟后，我的手心开始冒汗，因为要想锁定这份未来的友谊，我得从这初识的愉快浅聊，进展到设法取得她的联系方式，但这个过渡必定会是尴尬的。	在他离开我去自助餐台，在盘子里堆满公共素食墨西哥卷饼的时候，一个看起来很酷的女性走过来向我介绍自己，她有着闪亮的刘海和有意思的眼镜（优点），抱着一个哭泣的小宝宝（缺点），穿着露丝·贝德·金斯伯格的服装（不好不坏）。我们一拍即合。几分钟后，我开始手心出汗，我估摸着，从愉快的介绍性谈话，到我可以获得她的联系方式以锁定未来友谊的方法，肯定是个尴尬的过渡。

The Interpretation System of African Languages in the Senegalese Parliament Debates

First Jean Christophe Faye
Cheikh Anta Diop University/ Dakar- Senega
jeanbbchrist@gmail.com

Abstract

The present work deals with the interpretation system of local languages in the Senegalese parliament. In other words, it is devoted to the implementation of the simultaneous interpretation system in the Senegalese Parliament debates. The Senegalese parliament, in cooperation with the European Parliament and the European Union, implemented, some years ago, a system of interpretation devoted to translating (into) six local languages. But what does the interpretation system consist in? What motivates the choice of six local languages and not more or less than six? Why does the Senegalese parliament implement such system in a country whose official language is French? What are the linguistic consequences of this interpretation system on the local and foreign languages spoken in the Senegalese parliament? How is the recruitment of interpreters done? To answer these questions, we have explored the documents and writings related to the implementation of the simultaneous interpretation system in the Senegalese parliament, in particular, and of the interpretation system, in general. Field surveys as well as interviews of some deputies, some interpreters and other people from the administration have also been organized and analyzed in this study. This research has helped us have a lot of information and collect data for the corpus. After the data collection, we have moved on to data analysis and we have ended up with results that we have presented in the body of the text.

Key-words: interpretation, language, local, system, implementation

1 Introduction

Language had been a barrier in the Senegalese Parliament debates for several years, for some members of the parliament could not speak French, the official language or the other local languages spoken in the Hemicycle. This, not only, constituted a great problem of understanding and participation of the debates, but it also caused confusion and problem between some deputies. The administration was also confronted with some difficulties when translating or transcribing words, ideas or speeches uttered in a few local languages when they recorded the debates. It is in this perspective that the Senegalese Parliament, in cooperation with the European Union and the European Parliament, implemented a system of simultaneous interpretation in the Senegalese national parliament debates in 2014. The system consists in interpreting and translating into/from six local languages all the debates during the sessions. These local languages belong to the Negro-African language family. The implementation of the simultaneous interpretation system in the Senegalese Parliament debates, aims to strengthen the democracy and allow each member of the parliament to be understood and to understand what is said in French if they cannot speak it and in other spoken local languages in the Hemicycle.

At the launching of the project, Dominique Dellicour, the then Ambassador and Head of the European Union Delegation in Senegal, informed that the simultaneous interpretation system is a tool to translate, into six local languages, the debates in the Hemicycle. In cooperation with the European Parliament, the European Union (EU) co-financed this interpretation system with the National Senegalese Parliament. Dominique Dellicour informs that the help from the European Development Fund has allowed the acquisition of seven mobile booths fully equipped with audio and sound equipment. To sustain this investment, she says that it's important to set up an administrative structure responsible for the Interpreters.

According to Penda Ndiaye Cisse, manager of the EU supporting project, on behalf of the Parliamentary Institution, the project is managed, as

Proceedings of the First NLP4TIA Workshop, pages 32–38
Varna, Sep 8, 2023
https://doi.org/10.26615/978-954-452-091-5_005

the decentralized model, by a manager, an accountant made available by the authorizing officer of the Ministry of Economy, Finance and Planning etc. During the launching ceremony, Moustapha Niasse, the then President of the Parliament said that, from that day, any Member can have, in the Parliament, intervened in his / her mother tongue or local language they know best and be understood by all. Facing the satisfaction of his colleagues, deputies and chairmen of parliamentary groups, Niasse said that from then on, thanks to this system, every member has been able to listen and understand his or her colleagues, through his or her own language or French language.

Thus, the current work aims to analyze this system of simultaneous interpretation of African local languages in the Senegalese Hemicycle. In other words, it targets to show the importance of local languages in the parliament debates. In addition, the work highlights the linguistic consequences of the system on the foreign (French) and local languages. It is also devoted to the promotion of local languages around the world. However, to write the paper, a lot research has been conducted on the interpretation system and field surveys as well as interviews of some deputies, some interpreters and other people from the Senegalese Parliament administration have also been organized and analyzed in the study. This research has helped us have a lot of information and collect data that are composed of first and second hand data. So, the work is divided into four parts. The first part is devoted to the objectives and advantages of the implementation of the interpretation system. The second one is about the (six) chosen local languages and the interpreters and the third part deals with the linguistic consequences of the system. As for the last part, it lays the emphasis on the difficulties encountered by the interpreters and the deputies during the debates.

2 Objectives and Advantages

The implementation of the simultaneous interpretation system in the Senegalese Parliament debates, aims to strengthen the internal democracy. It allows each deputy to understand what is said in French or in other local spoken languages if they cannot speak these languages. The Senegalese Parliament has taken a major step as part of its mission of national representation. With the new simultaneous interpretation system in the Hemicycle debates, the language barriers are forever overcome. The interpretation system of local languages also helps each member of the Parliament to intervene in their mother tongue or in the local language they know best and be understood by the others. Thus, thanks to this system, every member can listen and understand their colleagues' speeches, through their own language or through the French language.

In addition, using local languages in the Hemicycle debates occupies a very important place in the dynamics of promoting these African languages. Beyond facilitating exchanges and conversations and discussions between members, this simultaneous interpretation system allows the Senegalese people who are represented by the deputies in the parliament to follow and understand the various interventions of the deputies in their native languages, mainly during deliberations and decision makings. It, furthermore, helps the members of the parliament to be able to have the latest electronic votes instead of hands-raising for or against votes (even if they do not use the electronic vote for their own raisons). Thus, the system is very significant because it allows the Senegalese Parliament to be equipped with sophisticated equipment, a tool that impacts on the quality of debates between representatives of the people. It also helps all the deputies to ensure their mission of regulators and controllers of the government action.

3 The Choice of Languages and Interpreters

The simultaneous interpretation system consists of twenty one (21) interpreters and seven booths in French, Seereer, Wolof, Joola, Pular, Soninke and Mandinka. The Interpreters were selected through a call for application. Graduates of higher education, with knowledge of two or more than two of local languages, have been selected following a call for applications. They have undergone intensive training of nine months in interpretation and translation techniques and have been dispatched into seven booths, three for each language, regarding their mother tongue or their first language (A language). However, all these selected interpreters have good knowledge of French language. As for the languages, six local languages that are Seereer, Wolof, Joola, Pular, Soninke and Mandinka are chosen thanks to the great number of their speakers in Senegal and their being codified.

3.1 Seereer

Seereer is a language which is interpreted in the Senegalese Parliament debates. It is a language spoken in Senegal and in some other African countries and whose origin and classification have given rise to a lot of debates within researchers in general and linguists and historians in particular. Thus, as Faye (2021:1) said in Possibility and Probability, several theses have been brought up for its classification and the main methods of classifying African languages, among other things, are to gather them in terms of groups, branches and families. This operation is essentially based on some comparisons of elements in terms of structures, phonologies, grammars, lexicon etc. of the current languages. However, Seereer language has linguistically been classified in various ways by many linguists and other scholars some of whom M. Delafosse, Cheikh Anta Diop, J. Greenburg, etc. According to the latter, Seereer is a language which belongs to the West Atlantic group of the Niger- Congo languages family (Greenburg: 1963).

So, belonging to the West Atlantic group, Seereer language has many dialects all of which are mutually intelligible. So, these dialects are divided into two groups: Siin (mainly called Siin-Gandum) group and Cangin group. However, it is the Siin Seereer language that is used in the simultaneous interpretation system at the Senegalese Hemicycle. It is more spoken in the center regions of Senegal.

3.2 Wolof

Wolof is also interpreted in the Hemicycle debates and is the most widely spoken language in Senegal, for the majority of the Senegalese people can speak it and may use it as a second language or as a lingua franca. It is almost spoken in all the Senegalese regions also in some other African countries. It is a language, like Seereer, that belongs to the West Atlantic group of the Niger- Congo languages family according the classification of African languages by Greenberg. It is composed of some dialects, any of which is spoken in a country or in a region or in some locality. It is used in literacy and in some formal education experiments. Wolof, a lingua franca of Senegal, is very vital in oral communication, in all acts of daily life, in the audio-visual press, in some religious sermons, in advertising, etc. Wolof is conquering new areas of use in the public life sector, debates on current affairs, training seminars for the nonformal sector, press conferences, etc.

3.3 Joola

Joola, like the two first languages, is among the interpreted languages in the Senegalese parliament. It also belongs to the West Atlantic group of the Niger-Congo languages family. It is a language that is spoken in the South of Senegal and is composed of several dialects. However, it is Fogny and Casa Joola that are used in the simultaneous interpretation system in the Hemicycle.

3.4 Pular

Pular language, also known under a variety of meanings (Fula, Fulani, Peul, Fulfulde, Fulakunda, etc.) is, as Seereer, Wolof and Joola are, a West Atlantic language belonging to the Niger- Congo languages family according to the classification of African languages by Greenberg. These Pular language diversity denominations, respectively used in different areas are mainly referred to as Pular dialects. Thus, Pular language is more spoken in the North and in the South of Senegal country. That being so, the interpreted Pular at the Parliament is the one regarded as the "standard Pular", meaning the one spoken by both the North and the South Pular people.

3.5 Mandinka

Belonging to the family of the Niger-Congo phylum, Mandinka is part of the Mandingo group in Mande languages. The Mandingo dialects are mainly spoken in West African countries. Mandinka is a dialect of Mandingo language mainly spoken in the South and in the East of Senegal country. It is among the languages that are interpreted in the Senegalese Hemicycle debates.

3.6 Soninke

Soninke is part of the interpreted languages at the Senegalese Parliament. Like the other spoken languages in Senegal, Soninke belongs to the Niger-Congo language family. It is spoken in the East and the Northeast of Senegal and in some other African countries.

All in all these are the local languages that are interpreted in the Senegalese Hemicycle debates. They have been chosen thanks to their status and their being codified. As such, they are regarded as national languages. Furthermore, they are the most spoken languages in Senegal with more than 95% of speakers among the Senegalese population. Thus, beside these local languages that have the status of national languages and are interpreted in the Hemicycle, there is the French language which is the official language in Senegal. All the debates in the parliament should be recorded in French even if they are uttered or interpreted in the local languages. However, the simultaneous interpretation of these African languages has some linguistic consequences on the local languages and on French.

4 Linguistic Consequences

The simultaneous interpretation system of local languages in the Senegalese parliament debates has some linguistic consequences on both local and French languages. The usage of local languages in the Hemicycle debates occupies a very important place in the dynamics of promoting these African languages. Beyond facilitating exchanges and conversations and discussions between members, this simultaneous interpretation system shows the important role of these languages in communication. However, the contact of these languages with French language brings about a language interfere and a codeswitching.

Local languages interfere when some deputies intervene in French and this interference is more remarkable in the grammatical, morphological syntactic, phonological, etc. levels. They (local languages) use the aspect (accomplished or unaccomplished) where French language focuses on tenses (past, simple present or future). This causes a problem of understanding to the secretaries, supposed to record the debates, and is reflected in their grammar levels. Thus, the fact that most of (or all) the interpreted languages are agglutinative languages also affects the speaking of French language, in the Senegalese parliament debates. The local languages words are made up of a linear sequence of distinct morphemes and each component of meaning is represented by its own morpheme; which does not exist in French and abates the deputies' understanding level. Thus, the formation of local languages' words interferes in the speaking of French in the Senegalese hemicycle. The local languages under study are agglutinative languages. Agglutination is a grammatical process in which words are composed of a sequence of morphemes (meaningful word elements), each of which represents not more than a single grammatical category. This term is traditionally employed in the typological classification of languages. So, an agglutinative language is a language in which words are made up of a linear sequence of distinct morphemes and each component of meaning is represented by its own morpheme.

The structure of sentences in the local languages under study also constitutes a focal point in the learning or speaking of French in the Senegalese parliament in so far as they (local languages and French) do not structure their words or sentences in the same way. The definite form can be an illustration of it, for it (definite form) is always placed after the determined noun in Seereer and Wolof, for examples, whereas in French it always comes before the noun it determines. In addition, in these local languages, the definite form is a compound form, each morpheme of which has its own function and there is no difference as far as the gender of the determiner is concerned. This pushes some members of the parliament to misuse the French articles when speaking and writing. The pronunciation of words, furthermore, interferes when some deputies speak French, for there are some sounds that exist in this foreign language but do not exist in local languages and their pronunciation causes some difficulties to the representors who have a weak level in French.

Some linguistic consequences have also been noticed in the phonological level of some deputies' speeches. Phonology is the branch of linguistics concerned with the study of speech sounds with reference to their distribution and patterning. It aims to discover the principles that govern the way sounds are organized in languages and to explain the variations that occur. This study of speech sound is very remarkable in the speaking of French as a foreign language in the hemicycle. Some local languages sounds interfere when some representors take the floor.

There are some sounds ($/v/$, $/z/$, $/f/$, etc.) in French language that do not exist in the studied local languages; which causes difficulties of their pronunciations. Some deputies face these problems and tend to use local pronunciation for these sounds. For $/v/$ sound they say $/w/$ and for $/z/$ they say $/s/$ and for $/f/$ they often say $/s/$. In addition, there are some letters that exist in all these languages but whose pronunciations are different. It is the case of the letter "c", which is pronounced /s/ or $/k/$ in French, depending on the following letters. But in local languages, it is pronounced like $/tf/$ in all cases; in other words, whatever the following letters may be. The pronunciation of "s" in mid or final position also causes some confusion and misunderstanding, for it is pronounced /z/ when it is placed between two vowels (mid position). When it is in initial position or between a consonant and a vowel or preceded by a voiceless sound, it is pronounced /s/. In the local languages under study, it is pronounced /s/ whatever its position in the sentence may be.

French language also uses double consonants such as "ch", "th", etc. in initial position, whereas our local languages do not use double consonants in such position. However, Wolof language, for example, can use double consonants in final position. Ex: jàmm (peace), lakk (burn). Unlike Wolof, the other local languages like Seereer do not use double consonants at all. In other words, Seereer language uses double consonants neither in initial position nor in mid or final position. So, the fact that the interpreted local languages do not use double consonants in initial position causes a lot of pronunciation difficulties when some deputies speak French.

5 Difficulties and challenges of the system

The interpretation system of local languages in the Hemicycle debates occupies a very important place in the dynamics of promoting these African languages. Beyond facilitating exchanges, conversations and discussions between members, this simultaneous interpretation system allows the Senegalese people who are represented by the deputies in the parliament to follow and understand the various interventions of the deputies in their native languages, mainly during deliberations and decision makings.

However, the members of the parliament face some difficulties due to the logistics. The materials used in the interpretation do not, sometime, function as well. Some other difficulties have also been pointed with the headsets and some micros that creak during some sessions and mainly when a deputy takes the floor.

Interpreters face sometimes difficulties when a deputy speaks quickly due to the fact that they have to analyze what the speaker just says and deliver it to the audience or listeners in their native languages (when the speech is in French or other local languages) or in French (when the speech is in one of the local languages), while still listening to the next works of the speakers. This action requires much attention and excellent sensory and cognitive skills. That is, the interpreters have a lot of challenges. One of the biggest challenges in the interpretation system is that multiple processes take place at the same time. Interpreters start with listening and analyzing the speech, putting in short term memory efforts and then reproducing it in the languages of the audience. So, the fast pace of the speaker and unfamiliarity with the subject can make the process more difficult.

Another difficulty that interpreters of the Senegalese parliament face during debates is that while they are simultaneously interpreting the speaker's speech, they are also listening to the speaker's next phrase and analyzing it to deliver it in the native languages of the audience. This process continues until the speaker stops speaking, and their speech can last from three until fifteen or thirty minutes, depending on the speaker (when it is about a deputy or a minister) or on the type of the debates. All this requires strict concentration. The interpreters also have to make sure that they deliver the speech in the same style and tone as that of the speaker to ensure that the message reaches the audience in the right form. Moreover, they have to maintain the same level of fluency in the target language.

The interpreters in the Senegalese hemicycle also face some challenges related to mental and physical fatigue, maintaining accuracy, quick thinking, technical issues and cultural differences. The inability to understand the speaker due to the speaker's accent, ability to project, or delivery, but also to audio equipment failures such as a deficient sound system is, furthermore, one of the great difficulties that these interpreters are facing during the debates. Another challenge that they face is the long lasting debates mainly when they are voting for the budget. This budget vote can last three or four weeks. Undoubtedly, this can be challenging on them. They can be "on" constantly and their throats can get sore and they can get tired quite easily; which may sometimes take a toll on the quality of the service, especially for simultaneous interpretation.

In addition, the interpreters encounter difficulties related to complex or technical words. Some of the ministers of deputies use technical or complex terms. Eventually, there would also be words that would not be found in normal situations or that are specific to one of the Senegalese cultures. In this context, the interpreters have to know and understand the exact translations of these concepts. This is in order to get the meaning across to those who are non-native speakers. In order to get through this type of challenge, they have to learn these words and concepts. In other words, they are given the rapports before the debates and this allows them to practice and work on the transcriptions or translations of these words or concepts before the debates. The humor or mood of some deputies that pushes them to utter insults or cry over others or to quarrel is one of the challenges that interpreters are also facing in the Senegalese hemicycle debates. These can include a lack of fluency in a language, or the use of jargon or technical terms that the receiver is unfamiliar with and to overcome language barriers, it is important to use simple and clear language, and to avoid using jargon or technical terms that the receiver may not understand.

Interpreters also have to accurately and idiomatically turn the message from the source language into the target language without any additions, omissions, or other misleading factors that alter the intended meaning of the message from the speaker. The interpreters of the hemicycle are sometimes confronted to filtering, selective perception, information overload, emotional disconnects, lack of source familiarity or credibility, semantics and gender differences.

6 Conclusion

The implementation of the simultaneous interpretation system in the Senegalese Parliament debates has strengthened the internal democracy. It has allowed each deputy to understand what is said in French or in other local spoken languages if they cannot speak these languages. The Senegalese Parliament has taken a major step as part of its mission of national representation. With the new simultaneous interpretation system in the Hemicycle debates, the language barriers are forever overcome.

However, this system has some linguistic consequences on both local and foreign languages. Local languages interfere when some deputies intervene in French and this interference is more remarkable in the grammatical, morphological syntactic, phonological, etc. levels. They (local languages) use the aspect (accomplished or unaccomplished) where French language focuses on tenses (past, simple present or future). This causes a problem of understanding to the secretaries, supposed to record the debates, and is reflected in their grammar levels. Thus, the fact that most of (or all) the interpreted languages are agglutinative languages also affects the speaking of French language, in the Senegalese parliament debates. The local languages words are made up of a linear sequence of distinct morphemes and each component of meaning is represented by its own morpheme; which does not exist in French and abates the deputies' understanding level.

We have also noticed that through the implementation of the system the members of the parliament face some difficulties due to the logistics. The materials used in the interpretation do not, sometime, function as well. Some other difficulties have also been pointed with the headsets and some micros that creak during some sessions and mainly when a deputy takes the floor. In addition, interpreters face sometimes difficulties when a deputy speaks quickly due to the fact that they have to analyze what the speaker just says and deliver it to the audience or listeners in their native languages (when the speech is in French or other local languages) or in French (when the speech is in one of the local languages), while still listening to the next words of the speakers. Another difficulty that interpreters of the Senegalese parliament face during debates is that while they are simultaneously interpreting the speaker's speech, they are also listening to the speaker's next phrase and analyzing it to deliver it in the native languages of the audience. The interpreters in the Senegalese hemicycle also face some challenges related to mental and physical fatigue, maintaining accuracy, quick thinking, technical issues and cultural differences.

Acknowledgements

I thank all those who helped me write this article. May God bless all of you!

Bibliographical references

DELAFOSSE, Maurice, 1912, Haut- SénégalNiger, tome I, P. 235-236, Maisonneuve et larose

DIOP, Cheikh Anta, 1954, 1976, Nations Nègres et Cultures, Editions: Présence Africaine

FAYE, Jean Christophe, 2018, Quantifiers in Siin Seereer International Journal of Multidisciplinary Research and Publications ISSN (Online): 2581-6187

FAYE, Jean Christophe. 2021 "Possibility and Probability in Seereer Siin: International Journal of Linguistics, Macrothink Institute.

FAYE, Souleymane, 2013, Grammaire Dialectale du Seereer, Editions : La maison du livre universel, E.L.U. Dakar

FAYE Waly Coly. 1979. Etude morphosyntaxique du seereer singandum: parler de Jaxaaw et Naaxar. Université de Grenoble 3.

GREENBERG, Joseph. H, 1963, Some universals of grammar with particular reference to the order of meaningful elements. In J. H. Greenberg (Ed.), Universals of language Cambridge, MA: MIT Press

GREENBERG, Joseph. H, 1970, The Languages of Africa, Bloomington: Indiana University

LAPRADE, Pinet, 1865, Notice sur les sérères, Annuaire du Sénégal et Dépendances, P. 131

SAUVAGEOT, Serge, 1965, Description synchronique d'un dialecte wolof: le parler du Diolof. Dakar

WESTERMAN, Diedrich & al, 1952, Languages of West Africa, Handbook of African Languages, 2e partie, Londres, Oxford University Press

Ngambay-French Neural Machine Translation (sba-Fr)

Sakayo Toadoum Sari
AIMS Senegal
tsakayo@aimsammi.org

Angela Fan
Meta AI
angelafan@meta.com

Lema Logamou Seknewna
AIMS Senegal
seknewna@gmail.com

Abstract

In Africa, and the world at large, there is an increasing focus on developing Neural Machine Translation (NMT) systems to overcome language barriers. NMT for Low-resource language is particularly compelling as it involves learning with limited labelled data. However, obtaining a well-aligned parallel corpus for low-resource languages can be challenging. The disparity between the technological advancement of a few global languages and the lack of research on NMT for local languages in Chad is striking. End-to-end NMT trials on low-resource Chad languages have not been attempted. Additionally, there is a dearth of online and well-structured data gathering for research in Natural Language Processing, unlike some African languages. However, a guided approach for data gathering can produce bitext data for many Chadian language translation pairs with well-known languages that have ample data. In this project, we created the first sba-Fr Dataset, which is a corpus of Ngambay-to-French translations, and fine-tuned three pre-trained models using this dataset. Our experiments show that the M2M100 model outperforms other models with high BLEU scores on both original and original+synthetic data. The publicly available bitext dataset can be used for research purposes. [1]

1 Introduction

Differential access to information is a pervasive issue in both developed and developing nations, reinforced by physical, social, and economic structures. The problem is especially acute in rural areas, where the lack of communication technology such as the internet can severely limit access to information. Furthermore, automated translation tools face significant challenges in dealing with low-resource language pairs and morphologically rich languages, leading to limited cultural exchange and market integration for certain nations. A major contributor to this problem is the fact that internet research is primarily conducted in languages such as English, French, Spanish, German, etc. resulting in limited data availability for other languages. As a result, Machine Translation (MT) is heavily dependent on parallel text or "bitext," leaving speakers of languages with limited data resources or parallel corpora at a disadvantage when it comes to building MT models (McCarthy, 2017). To make the recent successes of MT systems accessible and inclusive, research efforts should focus on identifying and closing the technological gap between these languages that lack digital or computational data resources. Addressing this gap will require innovative approaches for data collection and processing, as well as the development of new MT models that can effectively operate with limited resources. The Ngambay language is one of such marginalized and low-resource language facing the challenges of information access and automated translation. As an example of a morphologically rich language, Ngambay encounters significant difficulties in finding adequate translation resources, limiting cultural exchange and economic integration opportunities. The scarcity of internet research conducted in languages like Ngambay further exacerbates this problem, leaving speakers of such languages at a disadvantage in building MT models. Bridging the technological gap for languages with limited digital and computational resources, like Ngambay, is essential to ensure inclusivity and accessibility to the recent successes of MT systems. This research aims to contribute to the advancement of NMT for low-resource languages like Ngambay, making strides toward more equitable access to information and linguistic inclusion.

[1] https://github.com/Toadoum/Ngambay-French-Neural-Machine-Translation-sba_fr_v1-

Proceedings of the First NLP4TIA Workshop, pages 39–47
Varna, Sep 8, 2023
https://doi.org/10.26615/978-954-452-091-5_006

2 Related Work

Machine translation is a crucial subfield of Natural Language Processing (NLP) that utilizes computers to translate natural languages. Recently, end-to-end neural machine translation (NMT) has emerged as the new standard method in practical MT systems, leveraging transformer models with parallel computation and attention mechanism (Zhixing et al., 2020). Although NMT models require extensive parallel data, which is typically only available for a limited number of language pairs (Surafel et al., 2018), some research has been conducted on NMT using rare African languages such as Swahili, Hausa, Yoruba, Wolof, Amharic, Bambara, Ghomala, Ewe, Fon, Kinyarwanda, and others. (Emezue and Dossou, 2020) introduced the FFR Dataset, a corpus of Fon-to-French translations, which included the diacritical encoding process and their FFR v1.1 model, trained on the dataset. In their 2020 paper titled "Neural Machine Translation for Extremely Low-Resource African Languages: A Case Study on Bambara," (Tapo et al., 2020) introduced the pioneering parallel dataset for machine translation of Bambara to and from English and French. This dataset has served as a significant milestone as it has provided the foundation for benchmarking machine translation results involving the Bambara language. The authors extensively address the unique challenges encountered when working with low-resource languages and propose effective strategies to overcome the scarcity of data in low-resource machine translation. Their research sheds light on the potential solutions for improving machine translation in similar linguistic contexts. By tackling the data scarcity issue, (Tapo et al., 2020)'s work contributes to the advancement of machine translation for under-resourced languages. (Adelani et al., 2022) have created a new African news corpus covering 16 languages, including eight that were not part of any existing evaluation dataset. They demonstrated that fine-tuning large pre-trained models with small amounts of high-quality translation data is the most effective strategy for transferring to additional languages and domains. (Nekoto et al., 2022), in their paper "Participatory Translations of Oshiwambo", built a resource for language technology development and culture preservation, as well as providing socio-economic opportunities through language preservation. They created a diverse corpus of data spanning topics of cultural importance in the Oshindonga dialect, translated to English, which is the largest parallel corpus for Oshiwambo to-date (Nekoto et al., 2022). Other works have also been conducted on African languages, and many of them have websites for data crawling, such as JW300 and BBC. However, there is currently no research related to the Ngambay language or any other local language in Chad, and it is difficult to find websites related to these languages, such as newspapers or other sources, such as JW300.

3 Ngambay

Lewis, Simons, and Fennig (2013) reported 896,000 Ngambay speakers in Chad and 57,000 in Cameroon (Wikipedia). According to (Ndjérassem, 2000) J.H. Greenberg's classification in The Languages of Africa places Ngambay in the Nilo-Saharan family, Chari-Nil subfamily, Central Sudanese group, and Bongo-Baguinnian subgroup. Tucker and Bryan classify Ngambay as Bongo-Baguinnian, Sara group. Lakka and Mouroum, closely related to Ngambay, share a fair amount of homogeneity, though they differ in vocabulary and pronunciation. (John, 2012) states that Ngambay is related to Western Saras, Kaba, and Laka. Ngambay is spoken in Eastern Logone, Tandjile, Moyen-Chari, Mayo-Kebbi, and Chari-Baguirmi prefectures. It is used as a lingua franca by other ethnic groups. In 1993, 812,003 Ngambay lived in Chad, with at least half in Logone Occidental. The Ngambay people call their language "tàr Ngàmbáí" or "tà Ngàmbáí". Protestant priests and missionaries helped many Ngambay speakers learn to read and write. They translated the New Testament and Bible into Ngambay, titled "Testament ge cigi" and "Maktub ge to qe kemee" respectively. Ngambay hymns include "Pa kula ronduba do Mbaidombaije'g". It is worth noting that a monthly evangelical magazine called Dannasur was published for several decades until its discontinuation in 1995, or possibly more recently.

However, it is regrettable that the transcription of Ngambay has not taken into account its distinctive feature of tones. Several studies have already been conducted on this language, including the work of Charles Vandame (Archbishop of N'Djamena before) titled The Ngambay-Moundou, which was published in 1963 (Ndjérassem, 2000).

4 Problem of Education

The economic difficulties of recent years have had a significant impact on the education sector of Chad, leading to stagnation or even a decline in the quality and effectiveness of the education system. School infrastructure has deteriorated rapidly, and there is a lack of motivated and qualified staff, with illiteracy remaining prevalent and gender disparities showing no signs of improvement. Although the primary school enrollment rate is relatively high at 86.85%, only 41.32% of students complete primary school. When compared with Niger, a neighbouring African country facing similar challenges, the data is disappointing, with Niger having a primary school enrollment rate of 73.43% and nearly 72% of students completing primary school. A recent sectoral analysis of the Chadian education system highlights several deficiencies, including low enrollment rates, a lack of textbooks and inadequate classroom equipment, unqualified teachers, and limited access to higher education. Therefore, several changes are necessary to improve education in Chad. The PAQEPP (Projet d'amélioration de la qualité de l'éducation par une gestion de proximité) project, funded by the French Development Agency, aims to address these issues, involving 50 schools in Moundou and N'Djamena. The project was scheduled to run for four years, from 2017 to 2021, and involved more than 700 teachers and nearly 55,000 students. However, due to the global health crisis (COVID-19), the project has been extended until 2023.

One possible solution to address such problems is the development of efficient Machine Translation Models that can be deployed on edge devices to help overcome language barriers, as many people face difficulties in accessing education. Creating high-quality datasets for research in NMT is crucial for building these models.

5 Data creation

In data creation, we utilized two sources. The first source was *The Sara Bagirmi Languages Project* which provided us with the fifth edition (2015) of the Ngambaye to French dictionary in PDF format. However, due to the complexity of performing web scraping on a PDF, we manually created a parallel corpus of 1,176 sentences with short to medium lengths from the most commonly used sentences in daily life using a Google form. The second source was *YouVersion Bible*, an online Bible translated into multiple languages, including Ngambay. Using R programming, we performed web scraping on the website, but the Ngambay translation did not include all the verses like the French version. We extracted up to 34,647 sentences, but there were various grammatical errors, incorrect and incomplete translations, and inconsistencies. To ensure the quality of the data after crawling, we gave the dataset to native speakers of Ngambay and other linguists, including the Association of People translating the Bible from French to Ngambay in Chad, to check for problematic translations, misspellings, and duplicated sentences following Nekoto et al. (2020). After quality control, we combined the two bitext datasets, dropped inconsistent and incomplete translations, and ended up with 33,073 sentences for use in this project.

The morphological characteristics of a language can have a significant impact on its sentence structure and complexity. Our analysis revealed that the Ngambay language has a relatively simple morphology compared to French, which contributes to shorter sentences and fewer words. In contrast, French has a highly inflected morphology, resulting in longer and more complex sentences with a larger vocabulary. These differences in morphology pose a challenge for Machine Translation systems, as they must be trained on parallel texts that are aligned at the sentence and word levels. Given the complexity of French and the simplicity of Ngambay, it is essential to develop effective strategies for handling the morphological variations in each language when building MT models. By understanding the unique features of each language, we can improve the accuracy and effectiveness of MT systems for languages with varying levels of complexity.

5.1 Data Split

Splitting our bitext data into training, validation, and test sets using a 20% split size is a common ML practice for creating reliable, precise, and generalizable models. After splitting, our sets had 21,166, 6,615, and 5,292 sentences respectively for train, validation and test. We used the Python package jsonlines[2] to convert our CSV files to JSON format to match Hugging Face's pre-trained models.

[2]https://jsonlines.readthedocs.io/en/latest/

6 Models and Methods

We have used three transformer-based language models in our experiments: MT5 (Xue et al., 2021), ByT5 (Xue et al., 2022), and M2M100 (Fan et al., 2021). Transformers are a type of neural network architecture that has become popular in NLP since 2017 (Vaswani et al., 2017). They are used in many cutting-edge NLP applications. Unlike RNNs, transformers use a self-attention mechanism to weigh input sequence importance when making predictions. The transformer architecture consists of an encoder and decoder, which can be trained for NLP tasks such as machine translation, text classification, and language modelling. The encoder produces hidden representations from the input sequence, and the decoder uses them to generate the output sequence (Vaswani et al., 2017).

6.1 M2M100

M2M100 is a large multilingual machine translation model proposed by (Fan et al., 2021). It uses a shared representation space and a pivot language to enable translations between 100 languages, including low-resource and non-Indo-European languages. The model outperforms previous multilingual models and achieves state-of-the-art results on various translation benchmarks(Fan et al., 2021).

6.2 ByT5

ByT5 is a byte-to-byte transformer model introduced by (Xue et al., 2022). It operates at the byte level, eliminating the need for tokenization and making it suitable for languages with complex scripts or non-standard formatting. ByT5 outperforms existing token-based models on benchmark datasets, including those with low-resource languages (Xue et al., 2022).

6.3 MT5

MT5 is a massively multilingual pre-trained text-to-text transformer proposed by (Xue et al., 2021). It is trained on a large corpus of text in over 100 languages and can directly translate between any pair of languages without relying on English as an intermediate step. The text-to-text approach and diverse training tasks contribute to its versatility and performance (Xue et al., 2021).

Fine-tuning pre-trained models on a new low-resource language like Ngambay requires careful consideration of the available data and the best approach to utilizing it. As noted by (Adelani et al., 2022), one effective way to fine-tune pre-trained models is to follow a process. It is essential to select a target language that is represented in all the pre-trained models. In this case, we chose Swahili (sw) as our target language since it is a commonly used language that is present in most pre-trained models. This allows us to leverage the existing knowledge contained in the pre-trained models and adapt it to the new African language (Adelani et al., 2022).

6.4 Hardware and Schedule

Our models were trained on a single machine equipped with 2 NVIDIA T4 GPUs, 32 vCPUs, and 120 GB of RAM. During the training process, optimization steps for M2M100, ByT5, and MT5 took an average of 5 seconds, 2 seconds, and 4 seconds, respectively, based on the pre-trained models and hyperparameter described in the section 6.5. We trained our models for a total of 133,080 optimization steps. The M2M100 model was trained for 1 day, 15:02:53.55, ByT5 for 1 day, 0:56:06.98, and MT5 for 20:46:36.98.

6.5 Performance Evaluation Metrics and Hyperparameters

In this project, we utilized BLEU as a means of automatically evaluating machine translation. BLEU evaluates the adequacy of machine translation by analyzing word precision, as well as the fluency of the translation by calculating n-gram precisions. This method returns a score within a range of [0, 1] or on a [0, 100] scale. We specifically implemented SacreBLEU, which provides dataset scores instead of segment scores. A higher score indicates a translation that is closer to the reference (Papineni et al., 2002):

Using the HuggingFace transformer tool, we fine-tuned pre-trained models with settings that included a learning rate of 5e-5, a batch size of 5, maximum source and target lengths of 200, a beam size of 10, and a total of 60 epochs.

7 Results and Discussion

This section will detail our training process, specifically discussing the data augmentation method we used to enhance the performance of our pre-trained models. Our source language is French (Fr), while the target language is Ngambay (sba).

Our experiment aimed to identify and select the model that performed best among the pre-trained models when trained on the original bitext data, then use the selected model to generate synthetic data. Of the three pre-trained models we fine-tuned, M2M100 achieved the highest Evaluation BLEU score of 33.06, followed by ByT5 with a score of 28.447 when trained on a sample of 21,166, as shown in Table 1. This can be attributed to the fact that M2M100 is a multilingual model trained on a diverse set of parallel corpora from 100 languages, including news articles, subtitles, and other publicly available texts. It employs a shared encoder-decoder architecture that can be fine-tuned for specific language pairs and integrates multiple techniques to improve performance (Fan et al., 2021).

7.1 Data Augmentation using French monolingual data

In their 2016 paper, (Sennrich et al., 2016) proposed a method to enhance NMT models with available monolingual data for many languages. The two-step process involves training a language model on the bitext data and then using it to generate synthetic parallel sentences for the NMT model by translating the monolingual sentences into the target language (Sennrich et al., 2016). (Tonja et al., 2023) proposed Source-side Monolingual Data Injection (SMDI) to enhance low-resource NMT systems. A language model is trained on a parallel corpus and used to generate synthetic parallel sentences by translating the monolingual sentences into the target language. Evaluations on several low-resource language pairs showed that SMDI consistently improved NMT system quality (Tonja et al., 2023).

We are tackling a low-resource language with little in-domain data for Neural Machine Translation. Thus, we use a method similar to (Sennrich et al., 2016). To generate synthetic parallel data for Ngambay-French translation we have used the fra_news_2022_100K-sentences.txt dataset from the Leipzig Corpora Collection/Deutscher Wortschatz, containing 100,000 sentences related to 2022 news (politics, sport, entertainment, etc.) because no monoligual Ngambay data exists, unless in hard copy, hence, input (Fr) monolingual source-side. We create synthetic bitext data from French monolingual data. We split the monolingual data into sentences, and perform noisy translation to Ngambay then combine the translated sentences to form a synthetic bitext corpus.

Algorithm 1 Generating synthetic bitext data & training

Require:
- Original bitext dataset: $sba - Fr$
- French Monolingual dataset: Fr_m
- Target synthetic dataset: sba_{synth}
- Synthetic bitext dataset: $sba_{synth} - Fr_m$
- Languages: Fr, sba
- Translation model: NMT Fr $\rightarrow$ sba

Ensure:
- Train NMT on $sba - Fr$
- split Fr_m into sentences
- generate synthetic sba_{synth} by translating Fr_m sentences using trained and saved NMT
- Combine sentences from Fr_m and sba_{synth} to create $sba_{synth} - Fr_m$
- Add $sba - Fr$ and $sba_{synth} - Fr_m$ to create new bitext data
- Retrain the model using the new bitext data.

In machine translation, a model is typically trained on original bitext data, and then utilized to translate a set of monolingual source sentences into the target language. This process generates pseudo-parallel training data, also known as synthetic data. The synthetic data is subsequently combined with the authentic parallel data to train and improved the model, following the self-training concept introduced by (He et al., 2020). This involves training a model on labelled data and using it to generate pseudo-labelled data, which is then added to the training set to enhance the model's performance (He et al., 2020).

We used French monolingual data to generate translations for Ngambay. We combined these to create synthetic bitext data (see section 7.1). Training our models on both the original and synthetic data increased the M2M100 and ByT5 model's Evaluation BLEU score by more than 11 points compared to the original data alone. The MT5

Models	M2M100	ByT5	MT5
Eval BLEU	33.06	28.447	22.12
Predict BLEU	32.6016	32.6016	22.0481
Eval loss	1.7661	0.5152	1.0874
Train sample	1166	24366	21166
Train runtime	1 day, 15:02:53.55	1 day, 0:56:06.98	20:46:36.98

Table 1: Result of Fine-tuning M2M100, ByT5, and, MT5 using original Dataset.

model's Evaluation BLEU score increased by more than 2 points compared to the original dataset. This result is consistent with Tonja et al. (2023), who used target monolingual data in self-training experiments. Table 2 shows that M2M100 outperforms the other two models with original and original + synthetic data. (Agostinho Da Silva et al., 2023) with their work "Findings from the Bambara - French Machine Translation Competition (BFMT 2023)" have used Cyclic backtranslation, aims to enhance the model's learning by utilizing both the training dataset and a monolingual dataset. At each step k, they encourage the Machine Translation (MT) model for each direction to learn from a combination of the original training dataset, sentences generated synthetically, and sentences generated by the MT model of the opposite direction from the previous step. This approach allows the model to benefit from the diverse data sources, leading to improved performance and robustness. They have also used M2M100 model (Fan et al., 2021) as their starting point due to its outstanding performance, achieving the highest scores. (Adelani et al., 2022) demonstrated this in their project entitled "A Few Thousand Translations Go A Long Way!", they created an African news corpus with 16 languages, including 8 not in any existing evaluation dataset. M2M100 adapts faster than ByT5, and in most cases, it outperforms the other models and this have been confirmed by (Team et al., 2022)'s results. The M2M100 model is capable of translating between 100 languages in a many-to-many manner, which means it can translate any language pair among the 100 supported languages. The model is trained using a novel approach called Cyclic Backtranslation, which enables the model to learn from both the original training dataset and a synthetic dataset generated through translation of monolingual dataset. By leveraging a large amount of multilingual data, the M2M100 model demonstrates significant improvements in translation quality for various language pairs. Hence, it consistently delivers superior results in most cases.

8 Conclusion

The primary objective of this study is to demonstrate the possibility of gathering data on Chadian languages, similar to how other African countries do, and utilizing this data to develop a Machine Translation (MT) system. Specifically, the aim is to establish an MT system for the Ngambay language as an example for other Chadian languages. By doing so, we hope to set a benchmark for the accuracy of Chadian MT systems. To achieve this goal, we constructed the first bitext dataset for Ngambay-French and fine-tuned three transformer-based models (M2M100, ByT5, and MT5). Our experimental results indicate that M2M100 outperforms the other models and that monolingual source-side can enhance the performance of all models. We believe that such MT system can be integrated into electronic devices to overcome language barriers. However, this work has limitations that future studies can address

9 Limitations

Challenges exist in developing Neural Machine Translation (NMT) systems for low-resource languages in Chad. Obtaining a well-aligned parallel corpus is difficult, leading to inadequate training in translation models. Furthermore, technological advancement in NMT focuses on global languages, leaving a research gap for local languages in Chad. Consequently, end-to-end NMT trials for low-resource Chad languages have not been conducted. Online and structured data gathering for NLP research in Chadian languages is limited, making it hard to acquire enough data for successful NMT model training. A guided approach was used with languages having abundant data, but this may not capture the local languages' complexities, potentially affecting model performance. The M2M100 model's generalization to other low-resource Chadian languages is uncertain.

Models	M2M100	ByT5	MT5
Eval BLEU	53.1034	43.0504	24.6858
Predict BLEU	52.6012	42.52518	24.4494
Eval loss	1.1236	0.2801	0.9246
Train sample	24366	24366	24366
Train runtime	1 day, 12:00:14.38	1 day, 13:36:28.15	1 day, 3:10:09.87

Table 2: Result of Fine-tuning M2M100, ByT5, and, MT5 using original + synthetic Dataset.

Biases in the sba-Fr Dataset used in the project could affect the model's accuracy and practicality.

10 Future Work

To address the limitations of our current study, future research can focus on several aspects. Firstly, our dataset predominantly originates from the bible, which may introduce biased religious references. To mitigate this bias, researchers can collect more diverse and general text data for the Ngambay language.

Additionally, exploring advanced techniques like circular Back-translation using monolingual target source-side and Meta-Learning for Few-Shot NMT Adaptation, as proposed (Sennrich et al., 2016) and (Kim et al., 2019) respectively, could lead to enhancements in both the dataset quality and the overall performance of the machine translation (MT) system. These techniques have shown promise in improving MT systems by leveraging additional data and adapting to low-resource languages like Ngambay more effectively.

11 Acknowledgments

We express our gratitude to the African Institute for Mathematical Sciences (AIMS) with the program African Master's of Machine Intelligence (AMMI) for providing us with high-quality machine-learning training and for supporting us throughout this project. We also extend our appreciation to Google for providing us with a Google Cloud Platform (GCP) grant that allowed us to run our experiments. Special thanks go to the AMMI staff for their assistance and support. Many thanks to Chris Emezue and Lyse Naomi Wamba for the proofreading and useful comments.

References

David Adelani, Jesujoba Alabi, Angela Fan, Julia Kreutzer, Xiaoyu Shen, Machel Reid, Dana Ruiter, Dietrich Klakow, Peter Nabende, Ernie Chang, Tajuddeen Gwadabe, Freshia Sackey, Bonaventure F. P. Dossou, Chris Emezue, Colin Leong, Michael Beukman, Shamsuddeen Muhammad, Guyo Jarso, Oreen Yousuf, Andre Niyongabo Rubungo, Gilles Hacheme, Eric Peter Wairagala, Muhammad Umair Nasir, Benjamin Ajibade, Tunde Ajayi, Yvonne Gitau, Jade Abbott, Mohamed Ahmed, Millicent Ochieng, Anuoluwapo Aremu, Perez Ogayo, Jonathan Mukiibi, Fatoumata Ouoba Kabore, Godson Kalipe, Derguene Mbaye, Allahsera Auguste Tapo, Victoire Memdjokam Koagne, Edwin Munkoh-Buabeng, Valencia Wagner, Idris Abdulmumin, Ayodele Awokoya, Happy Buzaaba, Blessing Sibanda, Andiswa Bukula, and Sam Manthalu. 2022. A few thousand translations go a long way! leveraging pre-trained models for African news translation. In *Proceedings of the 2022 Conference of the North American Chapter of the Association for Computational Linguistics: Human Language Technologies*, pages 3053–3070, Seattle, United States. Association for Computational Linguistics.

Ninoh Agostinho Da Silva, Tunde Oluwaseyi Ajayi, Alexander Antonov, Panga Azazia Kamate, Moussa Coulibaly, Mason Del Rio, Yacouba Diarra, Sebastian Diarra, Chris Emezue, Joel Hamilcaro, Christopher M. Homan, Alexander Most, Joseph Mwatukange, Peter Ohue, Michael Pham, Abdoulaye Sako, Sokhar Samb, Yaya Sy, Tharindu Cyril Weerasooriya, Yacine Zahidi, and Sarah Luger. 2023. Findings from the Bambara - French machine translation competition (BFMT 2023). In *Proceedings of the The Sixth Workshop on Technologies for Machine Translation of Low-Resource Languages (LoResMT 2023)*, pages 110–122, Dubrovnik, Croatia. Association for Computational Linguistics.

Chris Chinenye Emezue and Femi Pancrace Bonaventure Dossou. 2020. FFR v1.1: Fon-French neural machine translation. In *Proceedings of the The Fourth Widening Natural Language Processing Workshop*, pages 83–87, Seattle, USA. Association for Computational Linguistics.

Angela Fan, Shruti Bhosale, Holger Schwenk, Zhiyi Ma, Ahmed El-Kishky, Siddharth Goyal, Mandeep Baines, Onur Celebi, Guillaume Wenzek, Vishrav Chaudhary, et al. 2021. Beyond english-centric multilingual machine translation. *The Journal of Machine Learning Research*, 22(1):4839–4886.

Junxian He, Jiatao Gu, Jiajun Shen, and Marc'Aurelio Ranzato. 2020. Revisiting self-training for neural sequence generation. In *International Conference on Learning Representations*.

M. Keegan John. 2012. The sara bagirmi languages project. *Morkegbooks*. Accessed: August 2022.

Yunsu Kim, Yingbo Gao, and Hermann Ney. 2019. Effective cross-lingual transfer of neural machine translation models without shared vocabularies. In *Proceedings of the 57th Annual Meeting of the Association for Computational Linguistics*, pages 1246–1257, Florence, Italy. Association for Computational Linguistics.

Arya McCarthy. 2017. The new digital divide: Language is the impediment to information acccess. *HILLTOPICS*. Accessed: August 2022.

Mbai-Yelmia Ngabo Ndjérassem. 2000. *Phonologie du Ngambai, parler de Benoye (Tchad)*, volume 12/13 of *University of Leipzig papers on Africa (ULPA): languages and literatures series*. Institut für Afrikanistik, Univ. Leipzig, Leipzig. Includes bibliographical references (p. 71-74).

Wilhelmina Nekoto, Julia Kreutzer, Jenalea Rajab, Millicent Ochieng, and Jade Abbott. 2022. Participatory translations of oshiwambo: Towards sustainable culture preservation with language technology. *AfricaNLP*.

Wilhelmina Nekoto, Vukosi Marivate, Tshinondiwa Matsila, Timi Fasubaa, Taiwo Fagbohungbe, Solomon Oluwole Akinola, Shamsuddeen Muhammad, Salomon Kabongo Kabenamualu, Salomey Osei, Freshia Sackey, Rubungo Andre Niyongabo, Ricky Macharm, Perez Ogayo, Orevaoghene Ahia, Musie Meressa Berhe, Mofetoluwa Adeyemi, Masabata Mokgesi-Selinga, Lawrence Okegbemi, Laura Martinus, Kolawole Tajudeen, Kevin Degila, Kelechi Ogueji, Kathleen Siminyu, Julia Kreutzer, Jason Webster, Jamiil Toure Ali, Jade Abbott, Iroro Orife, Ignatius Ezeani, Idris Abdulkadir Dangana, Herman Kamper, Hady Elsahar, Goodness Duru, Ghollah Kioko, Murhabazi Espoir, Elan van Biljon, Daniel Whitenack, Christopher Onyefuluchi, Chris Chinenye Emezue, Bonaventure F. P. Dossou, Blessing Sibanda, Blessing Bassey, Ayodele Olabiyi, Arshath Ramkilowan, Alp Öktem, Adewale Akinfaderin, and Abdallah Bashir. 2020. Participatory research for low-resourced machine translation: A case study in African languages. In *Findings of the Association for Computational Linguistics: EMNLP 2020*, pages 2144–2160, Online. Association for Computational Linguistics.

Kishore Papineni, Salim Roukos, Todd Ward, and Wei-Jing Zhu. 2002. Bleu: a method for automatic evaluation of machine translation. In *Proceedings of the 40th Annual Meeting of the Association for Computational Linguistics*, pages 311–318, Philadelphia, Pennsylvania, USA. Association for Computational Linguistics.

Rico Sennrich, Barry Haddow, and Alexandra Birch. 2016. Improving neural machine translation models with monolingual data. In *Proceedings of the 54th Annual Meeting of the Association for Computational Linguistics (Volume 1: Long Papers)*, pages 86–96, Berlin, Germany. Association for Computational Linguistics.

M. Lakew Surafel, Federico Marcello, Negri Matteo, and Turchi Marco. 2018. Multilingual neural machine translation for low-resource languages. *Emerging Topics at the Fouth Italian Conference on Computational Linguistics (Part 1)*, pages 11–25.

Allahsera Auguste Tapo, Bakary Coulibaly, Sébastien Diarra, Christopher Homan, Julia Kreutzer, Sarah Luger, Arthur Nagashima, Marcos Zampieri, and Michael Leventhal. 2020. Neural machine translation for extremely low-resource african languages: A case study on bambara.

NLLB Team, Marta R. Costa-jussà, James Cross, Onur Çelebi, Maha Elbayad, Kenneth Heafield, Kevin Heffernan, Elahe Kalbassi, Janice Lam, Daniel Licht, Jean Maillard, Anna Sun, Skyler Wang, Guillaume Wenzek, Al Youngblood, Bapi Akula, Loic Barrault, Gabriel Mejia Gonzalez, Prangthip Hansanti, John Hoffman, Semarley Jarrett, Kaushik Ram Sadagopan, Dirk Rowe, Shannon Spruit, Chau Tran, Pierre Andrews, Necip Fazil Ayan, Shruti Bhosale, Sergey Edunov, Angela Fan, Cynthia Gao, Vedanuj Goswami, Francisco Guzmán, Philipp Koehn, Alexandre Mourachko, Christophe Ropers, Safiyyah Saleem, Holger Schwenk, and Jeff Wang. 2022. No language left behind: Scaling human-centered machine translation.

Atnafu Lambebo Tonja, Olga Kolesnikova, Alexander Gelbukh, and Grigori Sidorov. 2023. Low-resource neural machine translation improvement using source-side monolingual data. *Applied Sciences*, 13(2).

Ashish Vaswani, Noam Shazeer, Niki Parmar, Jakob Uszkoreit, Llion Jones, Aidan N Gomez, Ł ukasz Kaiser, and Illia Polosukhin. 2017. Attention is all you need. In *Advances in Neural Information Processing Systems*, volume 30. Curran Associates, Inc.

Linting Xue, Aditya Barua, Noah Constant, Rami Al-Rfou, Sharan Narang, Mihir Kale, Adam Roberts, and Colin Raffel. 2022. ByT5: Towards a token-free future with pre-trained byte-to-byte models. *Transactions of the Association for Computational Linguistics*, 10:291–306.

Linting Xue, Noah Constant, Adam Roberts, Mihir Kale, Rami Al-Rfou, Aditya Siddhant, Aditya Barua, and Colin Raffel. 2021. mT5: A massively multilingual pre-trained text-to-text transformer. In *Proceedings of the 2021 Conference of the North American Chapter of the Association for Computational Linguistics: Human Language Technologies*, pages 483–498, Online. Association for Computational Linguistics.

Tan Zhixing, Wang Shuo, Yang Zonghan, Chen Gang, Huang Xuancheng, Sun Maosong, and Liu Yang.

2020. Neural machine translation: A review of methods, resources, and tools. *AI Open*, 1:5–21.

Machine Translation of literary texts: genres, times and systems

Ana Isabel Cespedosa
anabelcespedosa@gmail.com

Ruslan Mitkov
Lancaster University
r.mitkov@lancaster.ac.uk

Abstract

Machine Translation (MT) has taken off dramatically in recent years due to the advent of Deep Learning methods and Neural Machine Translation (NMT) has enhanced the quality of automatic translation significantly. While most work has covered the automatic translation of technical, legal and medical texts, the application of MT to literary texts and the human role in this process have been underexplored. In an effort to bridge the gap of this under-researched area, this paper presents the results of a study which seeks to evaluate the performance of three MT systems applied to two different literary genres, two novels (*1984* by George Orwell and *Pride and Prejudice* by Jane Austen) and two poems (*I Felt a Funeral in my Brain* by Emily Dickinson and *Siren Song* by Margaret Atwood) representing different literary periods and timelines. The evaluation was conducted by way of the automatic evaluation metric BLEU to objectively assess the performance that the MT system shows on each genre. The limitations of this study are also outlined.

1 Rationale

Recent advances in Artificial Intelligence and MT have brought a new perspective to the ongoing discussion on the automatic translation of literary texts among academics. More specifically, the significantly improved performance of Neural Machine Translation has triggered a debate among translation professionals about the future role of the translators.

It has been demonstrated that MT delivers better results when applied to scientific and technical texts which lack ambiguity and provide a precise message (Moorkens et al., 2018). On the other hand, literary texts are rich in rhetorical devices, ambiguity, and precise a certain level of creativity, becoming a great challenge for the MT to face when translating this type of texts (Toral, 2018), and as a result producing more literal translations which do not convey the essential meaning of the texts (Moorkens et al., 2018). Nevertheless, the research on how feasible MT for literary texts is or on the development of new techniques to improve the quality of literary MT, has been insufficient. The related work has centred on determining the main factors of the use of MT as well as identifying the cognitive effects on the human translator when applying to its workflow. These studies have proven that MT is both useful and powerful tool used in the translation process and can enhance the productivity of the human translator (Toral and Way, 2015a; Guerberof and Toral, 2020).

This study has been motivated by the recent advances of NMT and by the fact that the topic of the application of MT to literary texts has been underexplored. In particular, this study seeks for the first time to:

- identify whether MT performance is influenced by the genre and the time period of the literary texts. If so, how and to what extent do these aspects impact the MT performance.

- compare the performance of three recent NMT systems on literary texts.

The rest of the paper is structured as follows. Section 2 discusses related work. Section 3 details the methodology used by outlining the data used

Proceedings of the First NLP4TIA Workshop, pages 48–53
Varna, Sep 8, 2023
https://doi.org/10.26615/978-954-452-091-5_007

and the experiments conducted. Section 4 reports the evaluation results and provides a brief discussion of the obtained results. Section 5 lists the limitation of this study and finally Section 6 presents the conclusions.

2 Related Work

Most related work has focused on the feasibility of MT applied to scientific texts. With regard to literary MT, the studies have been focused on the narrative genre and the cognitive efforts of the human translator when MT is applied to the translation workflow.

It has been proven that the use of MT in scientific and technical texts have enhanced the human translators' productivity (Toral and Way, 2014). Since literary texts exhibit more ambiguity and use literary devices to infer its meaning, the widespread view is that MT cannot cope with this type of text (Bellos, 2012 in Toral and Way, 2015a; Kelly and Zetzsche, 2012). Nevertheless, there are researchers who consider possible the use of MT for translating literary texts successfully (Salimi, 2014, Toral and Way, 2015a; Toral and Way, 2018; Matusov, 2019).

Genzel et al. (2010) studied the Machine Translation of a poem, considering its metric, length, and rhythm. The results showed that the format could be preserved, but it could not obtain the same quality nor preserve the meaning.

Voigt and Jurafsky (2012) focused on the referential cohesion in literary and non-literary texts and their outputs when processed by MT. They concluded that although literary texts had more cohesive references than non-literary texts and although MT was able to cope with them, the referential cohesion is a key factor for good MT performance. Richardson (2012) employed Microsoft Translator Hub in the translation process of a church to cater for the demand of translation into several languages, creating corpora and glossaries and resulting in a higher productivity.

Toral and Way (2015a) reported the results of a study on the applicability of MT to literary text taking into account how related are the languages involved (French, English and Italian; Spanish and Catalan). They proposed to fine-tune the MT systems to the different types of literary texts regarding their characteristics such as cohesion, literary devices, dialogue, etc. They experimented (Toral and Way; 2018) with an NMT system customised to translate distant languages such as English and Catalan and compared the results with the previous translations by an SMT system. They drew their study on previous research (Toral and Way (2015b)) where factors such as limitation and freedom of translation were taken into consideration.

Moorkens et al. (2018) studied the perception of literary MT (based on both SMT and NMT) by human translators. Six professional translators were asked to translate from English to Catalan in three different modes: translating from scratch, post-editing NMT output and post-editing SMT output. It was shown that human translators preferred translating from scratch literary texts, but considered useful the suggestions offered by the MT systems. In line with this work, Toral and Way (2018) also proposed to incorporate automatic systems to the translation workflow to help the human translator improve their productivity.

Matusov (2019) examined the challenges that NMT faced when applied to literary texts with English and Russian as language pair and reported better performance after fine-tuning the MT systems to this particular language pair. In another study, Kuzman et al. (2019) applied NMT to Slovenian literary texts with the results showing increase in the productivity.

Omar and Gomaa (2020) identified the challenges MT systems face when translating literary texts; they concluded the most typical mistakes are pragmatic, structural and lexical. Guerberof and Toral (2020) analysed the impact of post-editing and MT on creativity and literature, as well as the perceptions of professional translators on this issue. Kenny and Winters (2020) studied how MT used in the translation process affects the translator's voice. Finally, Fonteyne et al. (2020) evaluated the recent improvements of NMT systems when applied to literary texts aiming to produce coherent translation at a textual level.

Among the most recent work is that from Ruffo (2022) who questions the lack of inclusion of literary translators in the discussion on technological advances of the automatic translation tools. A survey was conducted to identify the perception of technology applied to translation by professional translators. Although professional translators are not reluctant to technology, the negative views mostly had to do with the use and development of translation tools applied to literature.

3 Methodology: Data and experiment

Four texts from different literary genres were selected to establish their impact on the quality of MT; this study also sought to determine if the time period of the literary texts could influence the performance of MT. From the prose genre, two novels were chosen: *Pride and Prejudice* by Jane Austen, and *1984* by George Orwell; the poetry was represented by the following two poems: *I Felt a Funeral in my Brain* by Emily Dickinson, and *Siren Song* by Margaret Atwood. See Table 1 for more details. Three 3 popular NMT systems were experimented with: DeepL, Systran and Yandex.

LITERARY GENRE	ORIGINAL TEXT	TRANSLATIONS
Narrative	*Pride and Prejudice* (Jane Austen, 1813)	*Orgullo y prejuicio* (José Jordán de Urríes y Azara, 1924) *Orgullo y prejuicio* (Marta Salís, 2014)
Narrative	*1984* (George Orwell, 1949)	*1984* (Miguel Temprano García, 2013) *1984* (Rafael Vázquez Zamora, s.f.)
Lyric	*I Felt a Funeral in my Brain* (Emily Dickinson, 1858-1859)	*Sentí un Funeral, en mi Cerebro* (Álvaro Torres Ruiz, s.f.) *Sentí un Funeral, en el Cerebro* (Marta Rosillo Moya, 2021)
Lyric	*Siren Song* (Margaret Atwood, 1974)	*La canción de la sirena* (Raquel Rivas Rojas, s.f.) *El canto de la sirena* (Andrés Catalán, 2013).

Table 1. Texts selected for the study.

In order to objectively assess the quality of MT performance, we implemented the BLEU score metric (Papineni et al., 2002).

To this end, we chose two human translations from different time periods for each selected text. The BLEU metric system was set up both at sentence level with *sentence_bleu()* function and at corpus level with *corpus_bleu()* function contained in the NLTK (Natural Language Toolkit) library, as well as a cumulative score is obtained by assigning a cumulative weighting of 4-grams.

In addition to the BLEU score, the most significant linguistic features of each text were described, and the approaches taken by both the machine translation and the human translation were compared and correlated with the BLEU score.

4 Results and discussion

The evaluation results calculated by BLEU suggested that the lowest (0.3 out of 100) and highest (39.79 out of 100) quality scores were both achieved by Systran. However, reviewing the questions put forward in the Section 1 of this paper, it is safe to consider the following results.

The MT system which achieved best performance out of the three was DeepL, estimating the average BLEU score for the four texts. Overall, DeepL system was capable of producing a translation similar to the human translation with a higher consistency and quality as compared with the other systems. Although Systran and Yandex made the same type of mistakes, Yandex was more consistent and closer to DeepL (see Table 2).

	DEEPL	SYSTRAN	YANDEX
Average score for narrative genre	21.98	7.51	22.76
Average score for lyric genre	30.14	26.95	26.21
Global average score	26.06	17.23	24.48

Table 2. Global and Individual Average Score for each MT system

As for the performance of MT systems on literary genres, a higher score was achieved on poetry as opposed to prose. Systran obtained the lowest score for George Orwell's novel resulting in the decrease of the global average score for the prose. On the other hand, Margaret Atwood's poem emerged as the work with the best MT output, followed by George Orwell's novel.

Therefore, according to BLEU score, MT fared much better on poetry than prose when compared to a human translation. See Table 3.

	DeepL	Systran	Yandex
AVERAGE SCORE (Classical literature)	15.07	14.55	15.25
AVERAGE SCORE (Contemporary literature)	37.05	19.91	33.72

Table 3. Average score for each text following the results of the 3 MT systems.

Finally, all three MT systems delivered a low-quality output on the older classical works (those by Jane Austen and Emily Dickinson) as see in Table 4:

WORK	1984	Pride and Prejudice	I Felt a Funeral, in my Brain	Siren Song
AVERAGE SCORE (for 3 MT systems)	22.08	19.13	17.16	38.37

Table 4. Average score according to the temporary nature of the works.

In summary, the MT systems were able to perform better on modern literature which is expected to have a less complex style. We conjecture that another reason for that is because NMT systems are usually trained on more contemporary data.

5 Limitations

It should be noted that the results and conclusions should not be taken fully representative due to the following limitations of this study:

- **Data size**
  This type of study ideally requires larger datasets, or a large corpus in order to be significantly and sufficiently representative for the data obtained. In this study, only four texts have been used, two of them are extracts of a larger work, so the results cannot be generalised. Furthermore, the BLEU metric requires a large number of references in order for the scores to be as accurate and objective as possible. If not, there is a risk of obtaining not-so-accurate scores, since the algorithm is based on the comparison of MT and HT options.

- **BLEU limitations**
  In addition to the shortcoming mentioned in the previous paragraph regarding the number of references needed, it should be noted that this metric has its own shortcomings if not properly implemented. The algorithm does not consider the meaning of the sentence or the language variations as it regards sentences as strings. In other words, the system could compare the MT with the HT that may not be fully accurate or may contain mistakes as well. It may be the case for a good MT system to obtain a low score if it has been compared to a poor HT. Despite these shortcomings and limitations, BLEU is still one of the most widely used MT metrics.

- **Corpus representativeness**
  The representativeness of a corpus is as important as the size of the sample. In this study the literary sources were selected on the basis of their genre and availability online. For a more thorough study, it will be appropriate to choose a larger number of texts with a greater range of linguistics features in order to study to what extent the MT system can cope with these translations.

6 Conclusion

The aim of this study is to analyse the performance of the MT systems selected for different literary genres due to the lack of literature that addresses this issue. It was sought to assess the feasibility of MT to literary texts to and revisit the generally pessimistic widespread perception questioning the use of MT within the workflow of the literary translator.

To this end, three NMT systems (DeepL, Systran and Yandex) were selected to assess the performance and quality when translating prose and poetry from different time periods. The results suggest that the best performing system on these texts according to our experiments was DeepL. This NMT system produces more coherent and similar texts to those produced by humans. In addition, the obtained BLEU scores show that: a) MT fares better on poetry and does not do so well on prose b) MT delivers better results on modern contemporary texts and does not do so well on older classic texts.

However, it is essential to acknowledge the limitations of this study as outlined in the previous section. In future studies, it will be preferrable to use larger and more representative data in the experiments. The BLEU evaluation metric could be compared and correlated with other metrics such as TER (Translation Error Rate) and WER (Word Error Rate) to.

References

Abdulfattah Omar, and Yasser Gomaa. 2020. The Machine Translation of Literature: Implications for Translation Pedagogy. In International Journal of Emerging Technologies in Learning, vol. 15(11): 228-235. https://online-journals.org/index.php/i-jet/article/view/13275/7151.

Ana Guerberof Arenas, and Antonio Toral. 2020. The Impact of Post-editing and Machine Translation on Creativity and Reading Experience. In Translation Spaces, vol. 9(2): 255-282. https://doi.org/10.48550/arXiv.2101.06125.

Antonio Toral, and Andy Way. 2014. Is machine translation ready for literature? In J. Esteves-Ferreira, J. Macan, R. Mitkov, and S. Olaf-Michael (eds), Translating and The Computer, vol. 36. https://aclanthology.org/2014.tc-1.23.pdf.

Antonio Toral, and Andy Way. 2015a. Machine-Assisted Translation of Literary Text: A Case Study. In *Translation Spaces*, vol. 4(2): 241-268. https://www.researchgate.net/publication/290209944_Machine-assisted_translation_of_literary_text_A_case_study.

Antonio Toral, and Andy Way. 2015b. Translating Literary Text between Related Languages using SMT. In A. Feldman, A. Kazantseva, S. Szpakowicz, and C. Koolen (eds.), Proceedings of NAACL-HLT Fourth Workshop on Computational Linguistics for Literature, pp. 123-132. https://aclanthology.org/W15-0714.pdf.

Antonio Toral, and Andy Way. 2018. What Level of Quality can Neural Machine Translation Attain on Literary Text? In J. Moorkens, S. Castilho, F. Gaspari, and S. Doherty (eds.), Translation Quality Assessment (1st ed., pp. 263-287). Springer Cham. https://doi.org/10.48550/arXiv.1801.04962.

David Bellos. 2012. Is That a Fish in Your Ear?: Translation and the Meaning of Everything. London: Particular Books.

Dmitry Genzel, Jakob Uszkoreit, and Franz Och. 2010. “Poetic” Statistical Machine Translation: Rhyme and Meter. In H. Li and L. Màrquez (eds), Proceedings of the 2010 Conference on Empirical Methods in Natural Language Processing, pp. 158-166. https://aclanthology.org/D10-1016.pdf.

Dorothy Kenny, and Marion Winters. 2020. Machine translation, ethics and the literary translator's voice. In Translation Spaces, vol. 9(1): 123-149. https://pure.hw.ac.uk/ws/portalfiles/portal/41374556/Kenny_Winters_Translation_Spaces_Article_accepted_24_April.pdf.

Evgeny Matusov. 2019. The Challenges of Using Neural Machine Translation for Literature. In J. Hadley, M. Popović, H. Afli, and Andy Way (eds), The Qualities of Literary Machine Translation, pp. 19-23. https://aclanthology.org/W19-7302.pdf.

Jonni Salimi. 2014. Machine Translation of Fictional and Non-fictional Texts. An examination of Google Translate's accuracy on translation of fictional versus non-fictional texts. [Bachelor Degree Project, Stockholm University].

Joss Moorkens, Sheila Castilho, Antonio Toral, and Andy Way, A. 2018. Translators' perceptions of literary post-editing using statistical machine translation. In *Translation Spaces*, vol. 7(2): 240-262. https://www.researchgate.net/publication/329263225_Translators%27_perceptions_of_literary_post-editing_using_statistical_and_neural_machine_translation.

Kelly Nataly, and Jost Zetzsche. 2012. Found in Translation: How Language Shapes Our Lives and Transforms the World. New York: Perigee Trade.

Kishore Papineni, Salim Roukos, Todd Ward, and Wei-Jing Zhu. 2002. BLEU: a Method for Automatic Evaluation of Machine Translation. In P. Isabelle, E. Charniak, and D. Lin (eds.), Proceedings of the 40th Annual Meeting of the Association for Computational Linguistics, pp. 311-318. Association of Computational Linguistics. https://aclanthology.org/P02-1040.pdf.

Margot Fonteyne, Arda Tezcan, and Lieve Macken. 2020. Literary Machine Translation under the Magnifying Glass: Assessing the Quality of an NMT-Translated Detective Novel on Document Level. In N. Calzolari, F. Béchet, P. Blache, K. Choukri, C. Cieri, T. Declerck, S. Goggi, H. Isahara, B. Maegaard, J. Mariani, H. Mazo, A. Moreno, J. Odijk, and S. Piperidis (eds.), Proceedings of the 12th Conference on Language Resources and Evaluation (LREC), pp. 3783-3791. https://aclanthology.org/2020.lrec-1.468.pdf.

Paola Ruffo. 2022. Collecting literary translators' narratives: Towards a new paradigm for technological innovation in literary translation. In J. L. Hadley, K. Taivalkoski-Shilov, C. Teixeira, and A. Toral (eds.), Using technologies for creative-text translation, pp. 18-39. New York: Routledge.

Rob Voigt, and Dan Jurafsky. 2012. Towards a Literary Machine Translation: The Role of Referential Cohesion. In D. Elson, A. Kazantseva, R. Mihalcea, and S. Szpakowicz (eds.), NAACL-HLT Workshop on Computational Linguistics for Literature, pp. 18-25. https://aclanthology.org/W12-25.pdf.

Stephen D. Richardson. 2012. Using the Microsoft Translator Hub at The Church of Jesus Christ of Latter-day Saints. In Proceedings of the 10th Conference of the Association for Machine Translation in the Americas: Commercial MT User Program. https://aclanthology.org/2012.amta-commercial.14.pdf.

Taja Kuzman, Špela Vintar, and Mihael Arčan. 2019. Neural Machine Translation of Literary Texts from English to Slovene. In J. Hadley, M. Popović, H. Afli, and Andy Way (eds.), Proceedings of The Qualities of Literary Machine Translation, pp. 19-23. https://aclanthology.org/W19-7301.pdf.

sTMS Cloud – A Boutique Translation Project Management System

Dilyana Ilieva **Tihomir Nikolov**
dki@mitra-bg.com support@stms.cloud
Smart Innovations LTD in partnership with Mitra Translations Ltd

Abstract

Demonstration of a Cloud-based Translation Project Management System, called sTMS, developed with the financial support of Operational Programme "Innovation and Competitiveness" 2014 2020 (OPIC) focusing to enhance the operational activities of LSPs and MLPs. The idea behind was to concentrate mainly on the management processes, and not to integrate CAT or MT tools, because we believe that the more functional such systems become, the harder to technically support and easy to operate they become. The key features sTMS provides are developed as a result of the broad experience of Project Managers, the increased requirements of our customers, the digital capabilities of our vendors and as last to meet the constantly changing environment of the translation industry.

1 Credits

After years of experience and tests of various project management systems, we found out that we need a system with multilingual interface, which in our case is EN and BG, and one that to be easy enough to navigate without the need to learn too long "How to operate with it". At the same time we needed it to be cloud based, to have its own mobile version, client and vendor portal, option to upload and download files, a flexible model of project management having the option to add a multiple number of services to a single project, and respectively tasks to them, detailed dashboard which to be able to provide the user with all due information about the workflow with logging in the system, generation of quick reports and direct invoicing. Well, we put a lot of efforts and invested quite a lot of funds, and we managed to create a tool unique for the Bulgarian market, that gives you everything you need to quickly and efficiently manage a variety of translation projects without taking a lot of time for setup and training.

The product exceeded our expectations and after 2 years of real tests, we can safely admit that without it we could be lost in workflow management. For those 2 years we managed to fix minor bugs and to add several new functionalities as vendors working schedule, CAT analysis estimations and other ones, so we now feel ready to introduce our boutique product to LSPs. I am confident that most of you probably have their own tool or use some of the most popular ones, but I truly believe that once you scroll through the demo on our site, you will like it.

Now I would like to demonstrate it in the next few slides, so you get a better idea and a look deeper what our small and enthusiastic team of PMs and developers created.

We all know how demanding our customers are, how fast they need language services to be delivered and what their requirements are. Respectively, we have no less requirements to us and our team. For this reason, it is often possible to feel your office or your thoughts scattered. If you need to organize them and always have access to a tidy office, then you need a suitable TMS.

So, you won't miss deadlines, you'll always keep the budget for the project, and what is the most important, you'll be able to arrange and manage the complex puzzle of all the resources involved in the translation project.

Only a few clicks on sTMS and you will be able to arrange all resources, deadlines, budgets and more in minutes. You can send POs to everyone involved in the team straight away, and the Vendors List will match the pre-selected criteria for the project.

You can quickly send a quote to the client and provide them with an access to the project, so they can check the status of their projects at any time. Finally, you complete the puzzle with instant billing and a quick reference.

Proceedings of the First NLP4TIA Workshop, pages 54–56
Varna, Sep 8, 2023
https://doi.org/10.26615/978-954-452-091-5_008

Why sTMS?

There are many reasons to choose it, but I will try to point your attention to the most valuable ones.

sTMS interface is in English by default. However, it is built so that the organization using it can add another language completely free of charge. I believe that this option is not to be underestimated. In our organization, users of both interface languages are 50/50.

Another advantage is that sTMS does not need another tool integration to manage all processes, which eases the organization operation significantly. It is completely independent and you can benefit from it from day one.

We tried to eliminate as much as possible the need for training how to work with our tool, and our observations were that if the PMs fully understands the interface language, then they can start using sTMS in no more than 2 days. In addition, we placed the operation manual in a very easy to access place on the platform, so that anyone who needs to consult it can do so in no time.

I suggest you to take a look at the demo on our website. You will see how easy to operate is and at the same time comprehensive and fun the sTMS interface is.

On the Dashboard you can monitor all projects and tasks due for delivery, so you can avoid any delays or missed deliveries. In addition, the Projects List may be filtered "Due today" which automatically shows you a list with projects due today. This way you are secured twice.

Finally, you should not disregard the flexible pricing of the product, depending on the needs of the client.

Here are some more benefits sTMS has to offer. The notifications section is quite a valuable feature that's keeping you informed of certain actions in real-time. Whether it's receiving alerts about a vendor accepting a job or uploading a file to a project, a customer creating a project from their personalized profile or sending a file for translation, notifications feature ensures you stay on top of every significant event.

We also incorporated a highly flexible QA checklist. You have the freedom to tailor it according to your own preferences and QA procedures.

We have introduced a hierarchical approach to streamline business operations as a whole. Project managers, account managers, and administrators have distinct roles and varying levels of access. The AMs enjoy additional functions and the right to approve vendor and client rates. Meanwhile, the administrators have full control, including settings and configurations.

Our project budget section - as soon as you enter the services and tasks, this feature swiftly calculates your revenue and expenses, ensuring you never make a costly error and exceed your budget.

The client and vendor portals are new for our industry. We'll explore their features in the next slides.

sTMS Dashboard is designed to provide you with instant visibility to your daily tasks upon login.

Tables with projects and services to be delivered are complemented by a table with tasks to be received from your pool of vendors. There is also a table that highlights pending offers from customers. You can see in real-time updates on newly created projects, as well as outstanding invoices and a list of vendors that are not available.

And just like that, within a couple of minutes, every PM has an idea of how their day will unfold.

The LSP Portal has many cool features, and we've tried to outline some of the key ones for you here.

Create and Manage User Accounts - first up, you can create and manage user accounts with different roles. We'll talk more about the roles of customers and vendors a bit later, but for now, let me just say that the main difference between PMs, AMs, and Admins is their access to certain features. The option to generate reports and creating user accounts is only available for AMs.

As for company user settings, languages, currencies, and other fine adjustments, only admins are allowed to make changes.

If you're an AM, you can create and manage customer or vendor profiles. But keep in mind, this particular feature is only available to users with an AM role. We understand how important it is to have accountability in HR, service management and pricing. That's why we've limited this feature to maintain a high level of control and responsibility.

sTMS makes it super easy for everyone to create projects, add as many services as you want, and break them down into multiple tasks.

You can even generate and send these projects to clients right from the system or via email.

Now, let me tell you about our handy file management feature. It allows all project participants to attach and download files. The PM can control who has access to which files, and the system sends notifications, both in-app and via email, whenever a file is attached.

With just one click, you can issue and send the purchase order (PO) to the vendor. It automatically generates all the task information needed.

In the end, PMs will appreciate the project quality checklist, as it can be customized to fit your quality procedures and standards.

We all know how important invoicing is, right? sTMS helps you easily handle your invoicing through the system. And let me tell you, this module has been developed in a really smart way, so that the system only lets you choose from approved services. Let's say you have a project with 5 services. You can invoice 3 of them now all in one invoice - and save the remaining 2 for later (when they are ready). The system displays the invoice on the project page for your convenience and you always have a reference of which services are yet to be invoiced.

The vendor self-invoicing option is also extremely handy. Vendors can log in with their own accounts and invoice the approved tasks themselves. Alternatively, you can also self-invoice them. Either way, you get an up-to-date cost report instantly, eliminating the need for additional accounting tasks.

Now, let's talk about reporting feature. sTMS offers detailed reports based on projects, customers, and vendors. And you can use multiple filters to specify exactly what kind of reports you need.

For your convenience, you can export the data from these reports, as well as lists of customers, vendors, invoices, and more, in CSV format.

We've already mentioned the in-app notifications. They make managing translation projects so much easier and hassle-free.

Now, take a look at this project sample page, involving two services. We are proud to say that our tool looks simple, but it goes above and beyond to provide you with all necessary features for efficient and effortless project management.

Check out this sample page of a task assigned to a vendor, as seen from the PM's perspective. You will notice all the project details, attachments, status updates, and something really important the History feature. This nifty functionality allows you to track all the actions taken on a task or project. You can see who did what and when, whether it's changing deadlines, adjusting prices, or other important updates.

Well, let's take a quick look at the Vendor Portal, where vendors have all the options they need to easily accept or decline tasks, keep track of the ones they've accepted, attach and download files, and create invoices for completed tasks.

But that's not all. Vendors can also manage their contact details, billing information, services offered, and pricing right from their portal. Another handy feature is the ability to add their days off. This immediately updates the system, so both the LSP and PMs can see who is available and when. Say goodbye to the unnecessary email notifications and the hassle of distributing this information within the LSP when someone is absent.

Also, the Vendor Profile dashboard is a quick and convenient way for vendors to get an overview of their job count, value and delivery terms. And here is an overview of the Client Portal, where clients can create and manage projects with no extra efforts, handle project files, receive and accept or reject offers, receive and review invoices, and also monitor the project quality management steps.

Equally important, clients can manage their own contact and billing details as well as the services they require.

And a couple of words about the Client Profile dashboard. It's a handy tool that provides a quick reference to the number of projects and services, as well as the current month services amount.

In this presentation, we've covered the essential features that you would find interesting. If you have questions and want to know what else sTMS offers, you can drop by for a chat on our stand or email us at support@stms.cloud

Leveraging Large Language Models to Extract Terminology

Julie Giguere Anna Iankovskaia

julie.giguere@andovar.com anna.iankovskaia@andovar.com

Andovar Pte

Abstract

Large Language Models (LLMs) have brought us efficient tools for various natural language processing (NLP) tasks. This paper explores the application of LLMs for extracting domain-specific terms from textual data. We will present the advantages and limitations of using LLMs for this task and will highlight the significant improvements they offer over traditional terminology extraction methods such as rule-based and statistical approaches.

1 Introduction

In the context of localisation projects, extraction of terminology is more often than not the first linguistic task we perform. This is especially true as the type of localisation projects handled by professional services tend to be higher in complexity and require more subject matter expertise (SME). The more general type of content is now handled with robust results directly with the use of neural network machine translation (MT) or LLMs. The importance of technical terminology extraction in various fields has long been established. Having a solid glossary of terms is helpful to have a basis to agree on with the relevant stakeholders ahead of doing the translation. It is a helpful tool for the linguists and it allows to control the quality of the localised document via the use of term base and Computer Assisted Tools (CAT). It contributes to information retrieval and knowledge management. In the context of other natural language processing applications, term extraction is useful for text summarisation, semantic understanding and other usage. This paper explores the potential of LLMs for terminology extraction, providing an analysis of their effectiveness in comparison to traditional methods.

2 Context

LLMs have emerged as powerful tools in part because of their ability to capture complex language patterns and context. The architecture and training process of LLMs such as GPT-4 by OpenAI, BERT, and others helped us identify their potential for extracting terms effectively. We considered different methods for terminology extraction using LLMs. Contextual word embeddings -using pre-trained LLMs to generate contextualised word embeddings to capture word semantics based on surrounding text and enable better term identification. Sequence Labeling tasks ran with LLMs such as Named Entity Recognition (NER) to identify and extract domain-specific terms. Domain-specific fine-tuning to adapt pre-trained models to domain-specific corpora to improve term extraction accuracy within specialised texts.

3 Goal

Traditionally, in the context of a Language Service Provider, the extraction of terms from textual data was done using a CAT feature. We use Phrase inbuilt term extractor in our regular workflow and for the purpose of this comparison. The list of terms is then cleaned-up manually by a linguist to eliminate words that are not useful and to then add some terminology present in the data but omitted by the automatic extraction. This step is lengthy and requires the skill of a specialised resource such as a terminologist or a linguist with the relevant

https://doi.org/10.26615/978-954-452-091-5_009

domain expertise. The main goal of this paper was to find out if the use of LLMs could lower the human effort needed in extracting terminology.

4 Hypothesis

Statistical tools are frequency-based. In this experiment, a word should appear either at least once or at least two times in the text in order to be extracted. With a minimal frequency of 1, this results in a big number of false candidates. Their clean-up might take significant time. On the other hand, the tool with a minimal frequency of two generates less noise but it also omits numerous valid candidates. It is expected that LLM will outperform the other two methods by generating the highest number of valid terms with a minimum of noise therefore reducing the human effort needed in the glossary creation workflow.

5 Methodology

For this paper we are comparing a LLM (GPT- 4 by OpenAI) with a statistical model (Phrase term extractor). Phrase was used in two modes:

- '411' – from 1 to 4 word-terms; minimal frequency – 1; shortest word – 1 character.
- '421' – same but minimal frequency – 2.

The terms were extracted with Phrase 411, Phrase 421 and GPT-4 from three text samples and covering three domains: legal, medical, technical. Then, we also performed a manual extraction of the terms for each text sample and domain using a human specialist. This human extraction serves as a reference to identify the correct list of terms that should feature in the glossary. For each term extraction method, the number of correctly extracted terms (defined as a term also present in the list created by the human specialist) was divided by the total number of candidates proposed by the tool. The tools were compared based on the obtained accuracy score.

Prompt for the LLM extraction: content = "Extract domain-specific terms (domain: " + domain+") from the provided "+language+" text. \nText: "+text+"\nPlease extract only terms that are directly related to "+domain + " AND are present in the text (do NOT make up new terms, only extract existing ones in the text). Keep the same grammatical form and capitalization as these terms have in the text. Do not enumerate them in the output.``

6 Results

LLM got the highest accuracy score among the three tools (see Table 1). It generated one false term for technical (the term was not an existing term) and omitted some valid terms. Nevertheless its 'valid candidates vs. noise' coefficient was the best. We have been able to test in live projects and measure the saving in terms of human effort to clean up and finalise the list of extracted terms produced by the LLM-based approach versus the list of terms produced by the statistical model that are normally embedded into CAT software. This saving is important in the context of an LSP as it allows to be more competitive and to save time on the project's timeline. Several case studies showcased the successful application of LLMs in extracting technical terminology.

Content Type	LLM	Statistical '411'	Statistical '421'	Manually extracted terms	Text volume
Legal	21 correct terms / 25 candidates = 0.84	33 terms / 1,421 candidates = 0.02	16 correct terms / 183 candidates = 0.09	33 terms	504 words
Medical	52 terms / 66 candidates =	62 terms / 1,701 candidates =	9 correct terms / 93 candidates =	64 terms	487 words

	0.78	0.04	0.1		
Technical	41 correct terms / 56 candidates = 0.73	60 terms / 2,205 candidates = 0.03	24 correct terms / 288 candidates = 0.08	60 terms	724 words

Table 1 - Results

7 Advantages

LLMs is more efficient at capturing complex language patterns, handling polysemy, and adapting to domain-specific corpora through fine-tuning. They produce a more accurate and comprehensive terminology extraction.

8 Challenges and Limitations

LLMs may encounter difficulties in handling out-of-vocabulary terms, domain changes within the dataset, and they need significant computational resources during fine-tuning.

Conclusion: The LLMs term extraction has a great potential to improve the workflows and reduce the human effort needed. More work needs to be done to explore domain-specific pre-training and more efficient fine-tuning strategies to mitigate LLM limitations in technical terminology extraction.

We encourage researchers and professional service providers to adopt LLM-based approaches for technical terminology extraction to enhance domain understanding. We demonstrated in our results that LLMs outperform traditional methods. LLMs terminology extraction is a robust NLP application.

References

Chalkidis, I., Fergadiotis, M., & Malakasiotis, P. (2020). Assessing BERT's Syntactic Abilities. In Proceedings of the 58th Annual Meeting of the Association for Computational Linguistics (ACL), Online.

Devlin, J., Chang, M. W., Lee, K., & Toutanova, K. (2018). BERT: Pre-training of Deep Bidirectional Transformers for Language Understanding. In Proceedings of the 2019 Conference of the North American Chapter of the Association for Computational Linguistics (NAACL), Minneapolis, MN, USA.

Huang, H., Li, T., Liu, W., Wang, F., & Liu, H. (2021). Incorporating Domain-Specific Knowledge into Large Pretrained Language Models with Domain Adapter. In Proceedings of the 16th European Conference on Computer Vision (ECCV), Online.

Kageura, K., & Marshman, E. (2019). Terminology extraction and management. The Routledge handbook of translation and technology, 1, 61-77.

Lee, J., Yoon, W., Kim, S., Kim, D., Kim, S., So, C. H., & Kang, J. (2021). BioBERT: a pre-trained biomedical language representation model for biomedical text mining. In Bioinformatics, Volume 36, Issue 4, Pages 1234–1240.

Li, D., Xie, Q., Qiu, M., Xu, Q., & Wang, X. (2021). TPLinker: Single-stage Joint Extraction of Entities and Relations Through Token Pair Linking. In Proceedings of the 2021 Conference on Empirical Methods in Natural Language Processing (EMNLP), Online.

Xu, J., Zhu, W., Liu, P., & Zhao, J. (2021). Structure-aware Neural Model for Entity Relation Extraction. In Proceedings of the 2021 Conference on Empirical Methods in Natural Language Processing (EMNLP), Online.

ChatGPT for translators: a survey

Constantin Orăsan
Centre for Translation Studies
University of Surrey, UK
C.Orasan@surrey.ac.uk

Abstract

This article surveys the most important ways in which translators can use ChatGPT. The focus is on scenarios where ChatGPT supports the work of translators, rather than tries to replace them. A discussion of issues that translators need to consider when using large language models, and ChatGPT in particular, is also provided.

1 Introduction

ChatGPT is a conversational agent based on a large language model (LLM) specifically trained to enable users to have conversations on a broad range of topics in a desired format, style and language. Even though Open.AI released ChatGPT only at the end of November 2022, in less than 2 months it reached over 100 million users being considered the fastest growing consumer application (Hu, 2023). The emergence of ChatGPT may seem to the majority of the general population out of nowhere, but Open.AI has generated headlines in mainstream media in 2020 with GPT3, a large language model which is a predecessor of ChatGPT. Because GPT3 was able to generate texts in English that are difficult to distinguish from those written by humans, there was a general fear that it could be misused to generate misinformation, abuse, or produce student essays.

ChatGPT was built on top of GPT3.5, and more recent versions on GPT4, and part of its success comes from the fact that it operates a "freemium model" which means that many of its features can be accessed for free. This is in contrast to GPT3 which was available only to a limited number of users via an API. The fact that ChatGPT can conduct conversations in many languages widened its user base. One of the sections of this survey will provide a brief overview of how ChatGPT has been trained to perform better than its predecessors and give a non-technical explanation of how it works.

Recent months have seen a flurry of blog posts, YouTube videos and an increasing number of scientific articles which discuss a wide range of uses of ChatGPT from advice for healthy eating[1] and getting rich[2] to how to use ChatGPT to support and replace people in their jobs.[3] The fact that ChatGPT can handle multilingual text and can translate between languages attracted the attention of the translation industry, leading to renewed predictions that translators will be replaced by computers in the near future.

The purpose of this article is to provide an overview of how ChatGPT can be used by translators as a support tool and to discuss whether translators should be afraid of ChatGPT. While writing this article, it was difficult to decide which sources to use. There are numerous posts on social media and self-published articles on arXiv which can be relevant. However, because some are not peer-reviewed in any way, at times, their analysis is superficial and they contain speculations which are not supported by any data. For this reason, I will refer mainly to articles that have been published in peer-reviewed journals and conference proceedings, and to arXiv articles and posts that have generated enough discussion to consider that they were peer-reviewed in an informal manner.

[1] How to Create a Healthy Meal Plan Using ChatGPT https://www.makeuseof.com/create-healthy-meal-plan-using-chatgpt/

[2] Make Money With AI and ChatGPT: How To Earn $1,000 a Month https://finance.yahoo.com/news/money-ai-chatgpt-earn-1-143015520.html

[3] It should be pointed out that the inclusion of these links in the article does not represent an endorsement or recommendation. It is possible to retrieve many similar articles using Google and other search engines. These two links were selected because they come from more reliable sources and are likely to be written better than some other sources. However, this does not mean that their content should be trusted.

Proceedings of the First NLP4TIA Workshop, pages 61–63
Varna, Sep 8, 2023
https://doi.org/10.26615/978-954-452-091-5_010

Reports from market research companies like Common Sense Advisory[4] and Nimdzi[5] were also used to inform this survey.

2 Translation-related uses of ChatGPT

The rest of this extended abstract will briefly present the topics to be discussed in the full survey. A common theme throughout these topics is that ChatGPT should not be considered a tool that produces texts which can be used without human revision/checking. Instead it is seen as a powerful tool that supports, rather than replaces, its users (translators in the context of this article).

2.1 As a monolingual writing support tool

Part of the success of ChatGPT comes from the fact that it can provide support while writing texts. ChatGPT can function as a grammar and spell checker "on steroids", and it can rewrite texts in different styles. Given that ChatGPT was trained to be a conversational agent, the style of the text produced may not be appropriate in all the settings.

2.2 As a translation engine

Even though ChatGPT was not trained explicitly to translate texts, it proved capable of translating between languages. Initial experiments used simple prompts like `Translate the following sentences to [TARGET_LANGUAGE]` and showed that commercial translation engines like Google Translate and DeepL perform significantly better than ChatGPT (Jiao et al., 2023). More recent work, focused on prompt engineering to improve the quality of the translation (Gao et al., 2023). ChatGPT was also used as a translation tool that can help avoid gender bias, with better results than Neural Machine Translation (Castilho et al., 2023). A general observation is that the quality of translation is very different from one language pair to another. For example, Gao et al. (2023) report better results when the target language is English, whilst Castilho et al. (2023) observe poor results when Irish, a low resourced language, is involved. Small scale experiments conducted by the author of this paper seem to suggest that ChatGPT can translate noisy social media texts better than existing translation engines.

2.3 As an evaluation metric

ChatGPT was used to rate the quality of a translation using a prompt which contained the source sentence and the target. Kocmi and Federmann (2023) experiment with different large language models, including ChatGPT, and show they obtain state of the art results on WMT quality estimation tasks. They notice that quite often ChatGPT provides not only the quality score, but also an explanation for the score. Provided that the explanation makes sense, which is not always the case, this could pave the way to have explainable scores.

2.4 For terminology extraction

Given how good ChatGPT is at explaining concepts, it was proposed to use it for terminology extraction. Using prompts it was possible to extract terms, generate their definitions and translate them to other languages. To the best of my knowledge, no formal evaluation has been carried out to be able to say how well this approach works.

3 Discussion and conclusions

This extended abstract has discussed a few scenarios in which ChatGPT could prove useful for translators. The focus was on the application and output of ChatGPT. However, in addition to this, there are numerous other issues that should be considered when translators use ChatGPT such as privacy, hallucinations, speed and costs. All these issues will be discussed in the full survey.

The success of Open.AI with ChatGPT has pushed other companies like Google and Meta to release their own products and led to the availability of numerous large language models of different sizes and developed for different purposes. Open sourced models like Meta's LLama-2 are currently used by the research community to develop tools that can help translators either by translating content or by assessing the quality of translations. It is very likely that in the near future we will see tools based on LLMs that are more appropriate for translation scenarios, but they will require more specialised expertise.

References

Sheila Castilho, Clodagh Quinn Mallon, Rahel Meister, and Shengya Yue. 2023. Do online Machine Translation Systems Care for Context? What About

[4] https://csa-research.com/

[5] https://www.nimdzi.com

a GPT Model? In *Proceedings of EAMT 2023*, Tampere, Finland.

Yuan Gao, Ruili Wang, and Feng Hou. 2023. How to Design Translation Prompts for ChatGPT: An Empirical Study. ArXiv:2304.02182 [cs].

Krystal Hu. 2023. ChatGPT sets record for fastest-growing user base - analyst note.

Wenxiang Jiao, Wenxuan Wang, Jen tse Huang, Xing Wang, and Zhaopeng Tu. 2023. Is ChatGPT a good translator? A preliminary study. ArXiv:2301.08745 [cs].

Tom Kocmi and Christian Federmann. 2023. Large Language Models Are State-of-the-Art Evaluators of Translation Quality. In *Proceedings of EAMT 2023*, Tampere, Finland.

Author Index

Association for Computational Linguistics
209 N. Eighth Street
Stroudsburg, Pennsylvania 18360

ISBN 978-1-7138-9059-1

CURRAN ASSOCIATES INC.
proceedings.com